Consulting to Technical Leaders, Teams, and Organizations

Fundamentals of Consulting Psychology Book Series

APA FUNDAMENTALS OF CONSULTING PSYCHOLOGY

Consulting to Technical Leaders, Teams, and Organizations

BUILDING LEADERSHIP IN STEM ENVIRONMENTS

JOANIE B. CONNELL

 AMERICAN PSYCHOLOGICAL ASSOCIATION

Published by
American Psychological Association
750 First Street, NE
Washington, DC 20002
https://www.apa.org

Order Department
https://www.apa.org/pubs/books
order@apa.org

In the U.K., Europe, Africa, and the Middle East, copies may be ordered from Eurospan
https://www.eurospanbookstore.com/apa
info@eurospangroup.com

Typeset in Minion by Circle Graphics, Inc., Reisterstown, MD

Printer: Gasch Printing, Odenton, MD
Cover Designer: Naylor Design, Washington, DC

Library of Congress Cataloging-in-Publication Data

Names: Connell, Joanie B., author.
Title: Consulting to technical leaders, teams, and organizations : building
    leadership in STEM environments / by Joanie B. Connell.
Description: Washington, DC : American Psychological Association, [2022] |
    Series: Fundamentals of consulting psychology | Includes bibliographical
    references and index.
Identifiers: LCCN 2021032548 (print) | LCCN 2021032549 (ebook) |
    ISBN 9781433833731 (paperback) | ISBN 9781433837937 (ebook)
Subjects: LCSH: Science consultants. | Technology consultants. | Management
    consultants. | Leadership. | Organizational behavior.
Classification: LCC Q147 .C566 2022 (print) | LCC Q147 (ebook) |
    DDC 001—dc23
LC record available at https://lccn.loc.gov/2021032548
LC ebook record available at https://lccn.loc.gov/2021032549

https://doi.org/10.1037/0000270-000

Printed in the United States of America

10 9 8 7 6 5 4 3 2 1

Contents

Series Editor's Foreword

Rodney L. Lowman

The field of consulting psychology (CP) has blossomed in recent years. It covers the applications of psychology in consultation to organizations and systems, but also at the individual and team level. Unfortunately, there are very few graduate training programs in this field of specialization, so CP roles are mostly populated by those who came to the field after having trained in other areas of psychology—including industrial and organizational (I/O), clinical/counseling, and school psychology, among others. Yet such training is rarely focused on CP and psychologists, and graduate students have to learn through on-the-job training, reading books and articles, attending conferences and workshops, and being mentored in the foundational competencies of the field as they seek to transition into it.

After a number of years editing *Consulting Psychology Journal: Practice and Research*, the field's flagship journal, I felt that an additional type of educational product was needed to help those transitioning into CP. The Society of Consulting Psychology therefore partnered with the American Psychological Association to create a new book series. The idea was to create a series of monographs on specific fundamental skill sets needed to practice in this area of specialization. Working with an editorial Advisory Board, consisting of Drs. Judith Blanton, Brodie Gregory, Skipton Leonard (and initially Dale Fuqua and the late Edward Pavur, Jr.) and myself, our goal in this book series has been to identify the major competencies needed by consulting psychologists and then to work with expert authors to create short, accessible but evidence-based texts that would be useful both as standalone volumes and in combination with one another. The readers would be graduate students in relevant training programs, psychologists planning a transition into CP, and practicing professionals who want to add to their areas of expertise.

What constitutes fundamental skills in CP? The second edition of the *Guidelines for Education and Training at the Doctoral and Postdoctoral Level in Consulting Psychology (CP)/Organizational Consulting Psychology (OCP)*, created by the Society of Consulting Psychology and approved by the American Psychological Association (Gullette et al., 2019), the *Handbook of Organizational Consulting Psychology* (Lowman, 2002), and *An Introduction to Consulting Psychology: Working With Individuals, Groups, and Organizations* (Lowman, 2016) provide useful starting points. Each of these contributions was organized around the concept of levels (individual, group, and organizational) as a taxonomy for identifying fundamental skills. Within those categories, two broad skill sets are needed: assessment and intervention.

As with many areas of psychological practice, the foundational skills that apply in one area may overlap with others in the taxonomy. Interventions with individuals, as in executive coaching for instance, usually take place in the context of the focal client's work with a specific team and within a specific organization, which itself may also constitute a client. Understanding the systemwide issues and dynamics at the organizational level usually also involves work with specific executives and teams, and multicultural/international issues suffuse all of our roles. The APA Guidelines and the *Handbook* concluded, properly, that consulting psychologists need to be trained in and have, at least, foundational skills and experience at the individual, group, and organizational levels, even if they primarily specialize in one of these areas.

In inviting you to learn more about CP through this book series, I hope you will come to agree that there is no more exciting or inherently interesting area of study today than CP. The series aims to not just cover relevant literature on timeless topics in CP but also to capture the richness of this work by including case material that illustrates its applications.

Readers will soon understand that consulting psychologists are real-world activists, unafraid to work in real-world environments.

Finally, as one who trained and practiced in both I/O and clinical psychology, I should note that CP has been the one area in which I felt that all of my training and skill sets were both welcomed and needed. And in a world where organizations and the individuals and teams within them greatly need help in functioning ethically and effectively, in bridging individual, group, and organization-level needs and constituencies, and in coping with the rapid expansion of knowledge and escalating competition and internationalization, this book series aims to make a difference by helping more psychologists join the ranks of qualified consulting psychologists. Collectively, we can influence not just an area of specialization in psychology, but also the world.

ABOUT THIS BOOK

The technology space is expanding rapidly and is increasingly asserting itself in all aspects of people's personal and work lives. The types of organizations in which technical work gets done are many and diverse, ranging from mega-international companies to tiny start-ups. Consultants wanting to be effective in working with technical managers, work groups, and organizations need to know as much as they can about each of these levels of consultation. Imagine starting a consulting project in an engineering firm that builds immense buildings, bridges, and other structures; an early phase applied physics company struggling to move from a start-up to a company needing to be larger to survive in a highly competitive field; or a virology company under intense pressure to create a vaccine for a new virus that is rapidly disrupting the world and causing millions of people to die. In such work settings, the entry credentials are very high, people's worlds do not always center on other people, and the knowledge level needed to be effective in consultation may be expansive. Even for skilled consultants, there is a lot to learn to be prepared for work in this context. And what better guide for this journey is there than someone who started out her career as an engineer, worked in a technical firm, then earned a PhD in psychology (writing her dissertation on studying how technology affects communication at work) and who has subsequently spent much of her professional career working with technical managers and high-tech work groups and organizations?

This book is an unusual blend of the science and practice consultants need to be effective in this kind of consulting, but it also includes very practical suggestions and suggestions for further reading. In an unusual contribution, Dr. Connell interviewed a number of technical managers and consultants. She brings their thoughts and experiences to the book, which helps make the topics come alive and provides those with limited knowledge of this kind of consulting a first-row view of what to expect.

The structural approach to CP applies knowledge, skills, and abilities to be able to work at the individual, the group, and the organizational/systemic levels. The author explores each of these levels as applied to consulting with technical employees and managers, teams, and organizations. People who go into technical careers have many differentiating characteristics from those whose careers follow other paths (see Lowman, 2022). For one thing, technical work is dense, intellectually demanding, and requires intense attention to detail. It is inevitably highly specialized, and consultants may sometimes struggle to quickly grasp the basics of the nature of the work itself. Dr. Connell helps the reader better understand how people drawn to such roles work together in teams (spoiler alert: not always effectively) and in the kinds of organizations that are often found in the technical space. She demonstrates that although some generic consulting skills are relevant to this work, others need to be developed, especially when working in settings where the consultant's skill set may not always be appreciated. Like a travel guide to an esoteric destination, this book is a great resource for those learning to navigate consulting in the technical world.

REFERENCES

Gullette, E. C. D., Fennig, J., Reynolds, T., Humphrey, C., Kinser, M., & Doverspike, D. (2019). Guidelines for education and training at the doctoral and postdoctoral levels in consulting psychology/organizational consulting psychology: Executive summary of the 2017 revision. *American Psychologist*, 74(5), 608–614. https://doi.org/10.1037/amp0000462

Lowman, R. L. (Ed.). (2002). *Handbook of organizational consulting psychology: A comprehensive guide to theories, skills, and techniques.* Jossey-Bass.

Lowman, R. L. (2016). *An introduction to consulting psychology: Working with individuals, groups, and organizations.* American Psychological Association.

Lowman, R. L. (2022). *Career assessment: Integrating interests, abilities, and personality.* American Psychological Association.

Acknowledgments

Throughout life, I have learned that making significant achievements, such as completing a doctorate degree, earning a black belt in martial arts, or publishing a book, is not necessarily about being smarter or more capable than others. Rather, reaching the finish line relies more on tenacity. I have also found that tenacity is generally made possible by the support from family, friends, and colleagues; compassion from kind and giving strangers; mentoring from highly successful experts; and teamwork from the people involved. In other words, even though there is a single author on this book, it took a community to publish it.

I'd like to thank my family and friends, especially my husband and daughter, who have given me unwavering support. I am grateful to Rodney Lowman, the American Psychological Association (APA) Fundamentals of Consulting Psychology series editor, for encouraging me to submit the book proposal; for mentoring, editing, and responding at lightning speed; for paying attention to detail; and for making suggestions in a kind and educational way. I am grateful to Katherine Lenz, the project editor, for her thorough attention, encouragement, and responsiveness. I am also grateful to the rest of the APA editorial team and, especially, to the anonymous peer reviewers who provided valuable insights and suggestions for improvement. I am particularly grateful to Bernardo Ferdman, Gina Stetsko, Eric Roth, Adam Feiner, Etienne de Bruin, and the team at 7CTOs for their support and collaboration, as well as my own team at Flexible

Work Solutions, including Robin Stephenson and Alexa Samaniego. Finally, I am continually grateful to the technical, consulting, and human resources experts who participated in the research study for this book, who shared their wisdom for others to learn.

Consulting to Technical Leaders, Teams, and Organizations

Introduction

Before I became an organizational psychologist and consultant, I was an electrical engineer. I landed a job straight out of Harvard College at what at the time was one of the top companies in Silicon Valley. It was a dream come true for me. They moved me across the country and gave me a signing bonus that allowed me to put a down payment on a car and an apartment. I went from eating Top Ramen to having more money than I knew how to spend.

The California dream has continued through today, but the engineering dream fizzled out fast. I felt isolated and alone—there were so few women in the field—and I did not really know how to talk to anyone about it. I was not moved to control the machine as my colleagues were. It took several years and a lot of self-work to make the change to psychology, and I am glad I did. My mission when I went to graduate school in psychology

https://doi.org/10.1037/0000270-001
Consulting to Technical Leaders, Teams, and Organizations: Building Leadership in STEM Environments, by J. B. Connell

was to help engineers communicate better with each other, and that is essentially what I have done ever since.

Every consultant brings their unique strengths to their work, and I believe one of the reasons I have been successful working with technical leaders is because I "get" them. I am a very analytical person, and science is at my core, as it is for many of the clients I serve. My engineering experience gives me instant credibility, and my way of presenting psychological concepts tends to resonate with technical people. Obviously, a consultant does not need to be technical to empathize with technical leaders, but I hope that my explanations of how technical people think and experience the world in which they work will increase consultants' understanding of the technical leader's perspective and work context. You may be a consultant who is thinking about working with tech companies or getting into the life-sciences industry, or you may be a graduate student who is wondering where to do an internship, or you may already be consulting in a technical industry and are looking for tips to increase your impact. Or perhaps you've avoided technical industries because you do not have a technical background. Wherever you are, this book will help guide you to make inroads into technical industries and to have the maximum impact. The book will give you insight into the context of the technical leader's workplace and challenges, and it provides specific suggestions on how to work most effectively with technical leaders.

Chapter 1 focuses on the distinguishing characteristics of technical industries. I describe the challenges technical leaders face, along with the modifications in traditional consulting approaches needed to work effectively with them. In Chapter 2, I present excerpts from interviews with technical leaders that I conducted for this book so that you can "hear" their perspectives in their own words. The chapter also includes excerpts from my interviews with organizational consultants and human-resources leaders who work with technical leaders. Chapter 3 provides a four-phase consulting model for organizational consultants to use when working with technical leaders. I describe the first phase, attracting technical clients and winning them over, in detail. In the next three chapters, I focus on applications at the individual (Chapter 4), group (Chapter 5), and organizational (systemic) level (Chapter 6) and discuss how the model applies in each case. For example, for individual-level consulting, I address typical issues technical leaders need to work on and the types of resistance they may employ. For group-level consulting, I describe how technical teams are typically organized and the challenges that are common in these teams. I highlight specific types of technical teams, including self-managed teams, virtual teams, cross-cultural teams, and cross-functional teams, and I address specific team methodologies and contexts, such as Agile and Scrum methodologies used in software development, the U.S. Food and Drug Administration (FDA) approval process mandated for pharmaceutical and biotech companies, and compliance with standards. For consulting to tech organizations at the organizational level, I describe pertinent aspects of organizational structures, processes, and culture that are common in technical organizations. I also provide insight into how to develop effective talent management systems for technical people and address different populations within the technical fields, focusing on how diverse the technical industries both are and are not. In the final chapter, I raise current and future issues that influence consulting to technical leaders, such as the technology itself. I also highlight some things that have been missing from technical leadership research and industry initiatives and suggest ways to learn more about and improve leadership in technical industries. I close with suggestions for research and consulting endeavors to deal with the diversity challenges in these fields.

Throughout the book, I include fictionalized case examples that are based on composites of real people and organizations but have been disguised to protect client confidentiality. These examples are meant to illustrate prototypical situations that may arise for organizational consultants when they consult to technical leaders in various STEM (science, technology, engineering, and mathematics) industries.

On a personal note, when I was writing this book, I confided in my friend and esteemed colleague, David Beck, that I was worried what I was writing was not exactly "brain surgery." Exuding the wisdom from his 30-plus years as an organizational consultant, he responded, "A lot of what we do is not earth shattering. It's the skill of the consultant that makes the real difference." I was both relieved and humbled because it meant that this book is, indeed, another tool for you to use and your skill will combine with it to create the real impact.

One of the challenges that arises for organizational consultants when they try to work with technical leaders often occurs when the leaders brush off the consultants. Persistence is needed—one thing my experience with, and research on, technical leaders has taught me is that they both need and can benefit from working with organizational consultants. They especially need psychologically skilled consultants to help them become more self-aware, to understand the importance of focusing on the human side of work, and to develop the skills to lead and manage people. Technical leaders often have great impact on the world. They save lives, connect people to each other, and discover new ways to live. Helping them reach success in turn helps others and the world.

Technical leaders tend to be very smart, capable people. Some of them become very effective leaders. I aim in this book to identify general characterizations of technical people and their typical struggles, but I also note the wide range of personalities and capabilities within this group. Although analytical, disciplined styles tend to dominate STEM, creative personalities populate the innovative, entrepreneurial side. Many technical people have not had the occasion or inclination to self-reflect or have conversations about feelings, but others are highly self-aware and articulate. These people recognize the importance of our work, become champions for these efforts, and make great referrals to those who could use guidance.

1

What Differentiates Technical People?

The vice president (VP) of human resources (HR) at a medium-sized biopharmaceutical company reached out to an organizational consultant because she was getting complaints from high-level leaders in the company about the effectiveness of a team of director-level leaders in the research and development (R&D) division. She brought in the organizational consultant to coach the leader and provide team development to help the team build trust and collaboration, both within the team and across functions. She described the team of directors as all having PhDs and many years of research experience from their education and postdocs. A few of them had come to the company after prior work in other such organizations, where they had also been in research roles. The team members were all very bright, highly specialized in their respective fields, and valuable to the company because of the knowledge and experience they

https://doi.org/10.1037/0000270-002
Consulting to Technical Leaders, Teams, and Organizations: Building Leadership in STEM Environments,
by J. B. Connell

brought to their roles. They were doing great work in developing a new drug whose success was expected to launch the company to the next level or warrant a very profitable buyout.

The problem was, they were not getting along very well. Not only were they not getting along with each other, but they were also having conflicts with people in different functions. Responding to the complaints she had received, the VP of HR saw the potential for the dysfunction to impede the success of the company. She described the team figuratively as "a bunch of academics who all wanted to be first author on the paper." They wanted recognition for their contributions and were fiercely protective of their work because they were afraid that others were trying to take credit for it or take it away from them. The VP of R&D acknowledged that the team members were not behaving maturely and had bought into getting some help for them.

After contracting with the client, the consultant began assessing the team by interviewing each member and some others who worked with them. At this time, the organizational consultant uncovered evidence that a team intervention would not be enough; there was also an organizational-level issue of a culture of criticizing and intimidating and an organization-wide lack of trust and collaboration. The company had been started by a small team of researchers who had spun the company out of an academic research project. They had successfully secured funding to grow the company to over 300 employees, but they each had little to no leadership training or experience outside of academia. They were ill-equipped to manage and reluctant to delegate to the large number of employees they now had working for them.

This situation is not uncommon for technical organizations of all sorts. With the proliferation of technical industries, organizational consultants and HR leaders frequently interface with technical leaders. They also work with technical leaders in other sectors because the organizations they are working in have technical functions, such as IT, within the organization. If the COVID-19 pandemic has taught us anything, it is that technical leaders are crucially important to business success in almost all industries, and they are critical to leading the world in protecting and advancing humanity.

Technical leaders have gone from mostly supporting others in their endeavors to creating and leading corporations with worldwide impact. It is technological innovators and leaders who empowered the world to work from home, to have touchless financial transactions, to survive biological threats, and to develop new ways to connect with family and friends. The pandemic accelerated a trend that was long in the making; technical leaders are moving from the sidelines of organizations to the center, and they need to be able to lead people and strategy as well as technology (Hoving, 2007; Kark et al., 2020). Even before the COVID-19 pandemic hit, technical industries as a subsector were leading the U.S. economy. Health care and technology, for example, were the top two industries driving the economy in 2019 (Deutsch, 2020). Construction was third and life science was not far behind.

Not only are technical leaders running technical companies, but they also have become critical to creating the technology advantage for companies across all industries (Kark et al., 2020). Technological innovations are driving new ways of doing things, from farming to medicine to workplace communication to retail to investment to entertainment, and so on. Technical leaders now have more opportunities to lead business, and it is becoming essential for business leaders to become more technical to remain in their leadership roles. Collaboration between tech and business functions will likely be critical moving forward, as technology continues to evolve and dominate many aspects of our lives.

Technical leaders present both opportunities and challenges for organizational consultants. They are typically more highly trained in their fields of expertise than in people skills, and this difference presents many opportunities for leadership development and consulting on organizational and team issues as well. Technical leaders are also more often known for their independent thinking and for their distaste of being told what to do, especially by nontechnical people, and these traits can pose challenges for organizational consultants. This book addresses both the opportunities and the challenges for organizational consultants working in this area.

Organizational consultants and HR leaders themselves also increasingly rely on technology-driven tools and apps to assess and manage talent, track

HR functions, and provide services to employees and clients (Ihsan & Furnham, 2018). Artificial intelligence is already being used to provide some HR functions—for example, chatbots are used to facilitate self-service transactions and recruiting—and it is being considered for many more functions (Ernst & Young, 2018). Organizational consultants and HR professionals will need to collaborate with technical leaders to guide technology development; learn, integrate, and maintain the tools; and oversee privacy. In other words, they will need to work with technical leaders to keep their jobs and stay current.

Another compelling reason for organizational consultants to want to work with technical leaders is the public's concern for the growing lack of empathy and ethics in technical industries—and even worse, the possibility that leaders at the top of many high-profile companies may not care about the public's interest (Strobel et al., 2013). For example, numerous news articles have reported that tech companies have made billions of dollars addicting people to social media over a 20-year span starting in the early 2000s, while pharmaceutical companies made billions addicting people to opioids. Leaders in both these industries knew they were manipulating people and knew the outcomes were unhealthy, and yet they kept going. Tristan Harris, a former Google design ethicist, roused the tech community starting in 2013, as he accused the major Silicon Valley firms of "brain hacking" billions of people and created the Center for Humane Technology (https://www.humanetech.com/who-we-are). The Netflix original film *The Social Dilemma* also raised these concerns to the public (https://www.thesocialdilemma.com/). The opioid crisis in America, wherein pharmaceutical companies pushed OxyContin and other brands known to be addictive onto doctors, pharmacists, and patients, has also received heavy news coverage (Kornfield et al., 2020).

Organizational consultants can help technical leaders navigate the moral challenges of leadership (Emler, 2019). Lack of empathy can have far-reaching consequences, including the marginalization and oppression of people and the lack of interest in diversity, equity, and inclusion, as well as the design of the dehumanizing communication technology, health care, and other infrastructures we use daily in and outside of work. This is not to say that all technical leaders are sociopaths with feeling or compassion deficits—many are caring people who are trying to make the world a better place—but some very powerful technical leaders have been adversely affecting the lives of millions, even billions, of people. And even the leaders who want to do good things may simply be unaware of the impact of their behavior. Organizational consultants can help technical organizations by assessing leadership candidates to identify and advise hiring authorities about those with derailing personality characteristics and by coaching leaders who demonstrate a willingness to receive feedback and learn (Gøtzsche-Astrup, 2018).

For the purposes of this book, *technical leaders* are defined as people who lead organizations and/or teams in highly specialized technical fields, such as science, technology, engineering, and mathematics (STEM), and some high-level finance. STEM fields include astronomy, biology, chemistry, computer science, engineering, earth sciences, health sciences, information technology, mathematics, and physics (Moody, 2019). Some master's-level finance and economics programs are being recognized as STEM fields in universities as well (Redden, 2018).

TECHNICAL INDUSTRIES ARE DIFFERENT FROM OTHER INDUSTRIES

Research shows that technical organizations differ from organizations in other industries (Grenny & Maxfield, 2016; Vieth & Smith, 2008). To start, technical industries are continuously evolving, and they change incredibly rapidly compared with other industries, such as retail, service, and government.

These organizations also tend to be very complex. The nature of what STEM industries analyze and produce is often complex, multifaceted, and obscure. For example, Google's code base is made up of two billion lines of code, the human genome is made up of 3.2 billion sequence pairs, and around 630,000 companies are traded publicly throughout the world (Desjardins, 2017; Fuhrmann, 2019; National Human Genome Research Institute, 2019). These industries tend to require many highly trained specialists to work together and coordinate across functions.

It is often difficult for people outside of their fields, such as business partners, investors, and customers to understand what they do and what their needs are.

Cross-functional exchange can be a major source of miscommunication and conflict. In part, because of the complexity of the work, leadership can be fraught with ambiguity. Technical teams often have unclear, overlapping, and shared accountabilities. For example, as explained in Chapter 5, teams that follow the Agile philosophy may have three different leaders, such as a project manager who plans, leads, organizes, and motivates one or more Agile project teams and coordinates with upper management; a scrum master, who makes sure the team follows the Agile process, clears obstacles, and keeps outsiders from interrupting the team; and a product owner, who sets, prioritizes, and evaluates the work generated by the team to meet customer specifications. When these leaders are not aligned, they may have conflicting priorities, give different directions to the team, and communicate different messages to others outside the team. In addition, people from many different functions and disciplines work together to solve technical problems. For example, in drug development, teams may include biologists, chemists, physicists, mathematicians, and manufacturing and marketing experts, as well as people in research, development, regulatory, and other functions (Geoui, 2016). In addition to the many cross-disciplinary teams, there are many different phases of the research and many opportunities to hand over projects and accountability. As in any complicated organization, misalignment and competition between teams and leaders may further muddy the waters.

Technical industries experience intense competition for talent, and the professional communities in specialized areas tend to be small (Morris, 2019). Many technical people know each other and end up working together or for each other at different points of their careers in different companies (Development Dimensions International [DDI] et al., 2018; Grenny & Maxfield, 2016). For example, a LinkedIn study of annual turnover found that the tech industry had the highest employee turnover of any business sector—over 13% across all sizes of tech companies (Booz, 2018). Length of tenure was also short. Another study reported that the average length of employment was 1.1 years for Google employees, 1 year for Amazon employees, and 24 months for Apple employees (PayScale, 2020). In addition to high turnover, competition for talent splits the talent between two tiers of companies: the top tier of elite companies (e.g., Google, Genentech, Goldman Sachs) and companies with innovative and interesting projects (e.g., SpaceX, Pixar, Illumina), who get to hire superstars; and the lower tier of lesser known companies who struggle to attract and retain good talent to work on their more mundane projects.

Because of relentless competition and threat of obsoletion, technical industries tend to apply relentless pressure on their employees. People's jobs are intense and fast-paced, and there is what is commonly referred to in the industry as a "heroic culture" that rewards people who maintain few boundaries between personal and work life (Grenny & Maxfield, 2016). As a result, work–life balance, personal renewal, and sustainability are generally not highly valued or displayed.

There is mounting evidence that technical companies have less success growing leadership talent than other industries do. In 2018, for example, three major firms collaborated to conduct a very large leadership study that included business and technical leaders as well as HR professionals at all levels (DDI et al., 2018). The study included more than 25,000 leaders and 2,500 HR professionals in almost 2,500 organizations, including more than 1,000 C-Suite executives and 10,000 high-potential employees. The technology organizations reported only a 61% success rate for filling leadership positions internally, which was 20% lower than in other industries. Biotech, pharmaceutical, and other science-based industries experience very similar trends with both their scientists and leaders, as do the technical trades, especially in start-up companies (Banerjee & Cole, 2012; Gurdon & Samsom, 2010). Start-ups are mostly within the technology and health care sectors and fail more often than they succeed, largely from failures by the technical leaders to handle business challenges, such as managing funds, understanding the market, getting the right team on board, paying attention to customer needs, and simply having a clear business model (CB Insights, 2019; Perez, 2019).

VitalSmarts, another consulting firm, compared thousands of technical and nontechnical managers to learn how leadership challenges in the tech industry differed from those in nontech industries (Grenny &

Maxfield, 2016). They interviewed technical leaders and surveyed more than 3,600 people, divided equally between managers and employees, from tech and nontech organizations. They were surprised to hear during the interviews that very few leaders had been coached or trained on issues that affected tech leaders. The leaders explained that talking about leadership challenges was not acceptable in their company's culture. The Global Leadership Forecast (DDI et al., 2018) researchers found that technology organizations invested less in leadership development than did other industries. For example, tech companies invested on average 15% less on development for first-time managers than did companies in other industries. They also spent less time than other industries on leadership development.

DIFFERENCES AMONG TECHNICAL INDUSTRIES

Even though there are major similarities across technical industries, there are some differences among them. Organizations may differ based on their size and whether their mission is entrepreneurial or they are start-ups (Greiner, 1998).

Start-Ups Versus Larger Organizations

Since there are so many start-ups in technical industries, it is worth highlighting a few differences between the contexts of start-ups and larger organizations. Although start-ups and entrepreneurs vary widely, start-ups generally need a different kind of leadership and coaching than do organizations further along in their development (Berman, 2019). Many start-ups, especially ones with quite limited resources, need leaders who are more hands-on and flexible, who are innovative and resourceful, and who are good at finding opportunities (Frese & Gielnik, 2014).

Lowman (2016) described common characteristics of entrepreneurs that have been shown in the research. He found that entrepreneurs are typically more focused on creating things quickly than they are on navigating politics and pleasing shareholders. Entrepreneurs tend to employ creative, independent thinking to succeed more often than organizational leaders, who often need to conform more and collaborate across functions. Entrepreneurs also tend to be especially resilient and optimistic, highly confident, and able to tolerate ambiguity well. They may behave idiosyncratically because in a tiny organization, the organization is the people, and cultures are really the founders. As organizations grow, they need other skill sets; the organizational culture becomes less dependent on a single person or small group of people.

When working with rapidly growing start-ups, organizational consultants may get involved in helping to determine whether entrepreneurial leaders have the abilities and interests to lead the organization as it scales up to become a larger company. Some leaders have the capacity to develop into corporate leaders and may benefit from coaching and training. Others may be better suited to sticking to innovative roles, such as a serial entrepreneur, or leading R&D programs in the company. David H. Crean is a managing director and partner at Objective Capital Partners, a middle-market investment banking firm located in Southern California, where he leads the firm's mergers and acquisitions, partnering, and capital financing transactions with life science and health care clients. He has advised between 600 and 700 start-up founders in these industries. When I interviewed him for this book, he said,

> The biggest problem with these companies tends to be their management, the founders. Nine out of 10 entrepreneurs don't have the skills to run a company. The problem arises when they won't get out of the way and hire a professional CEO. A CEO does not need to know the technical stuff; they need to know how to run a company. The founders can then move into a chief science officer or similar technical role. (D. Crean, personal communication, January 7, 2021)

Organizational consultants can contribute by offering assessments and coaching to entrepreneurial leaders and helping them choose which path to take, as in learning the business and people skills necessary to lead the company or moving into a technical role and letting an experienced businessperson lead the company.

Scientific Research and Development

At its core, science is a field of research to attain new knowledge. The domains of science tend to focus more on discovering what exists and how things work than on creating new products, which is left up to engineers and other kinds of applied scientists. To summarize Britton (2010), engineers create; scientists understand.

Research is often conducted in universities. In fact, scientists usually learn how to conduct research in college and graduate programs, and most scientists have advanced (e.g., doctorate) degrees and often postdoctoral training. Science has traditionally been funded by governments and other not-for-profit agencies to further human knowledge. Some industries, however, also fund scientific research to gain competitive advantage by discovering new ways of making things. R&D departments are typically found in large companies that can afford to invest in the future. Start-ups may conduct research funded by external investors, but this research is typically not exploratory. Rather, it is targeted to problems that can be monetized. The life science industry, for example, conducts research to develop new therapies and medical devices to improve human lives. They typically do this with large upfront investments by investment firms or, in the case of the big pharma companies, they reinvest profits themselves. The aerospace industry is another example of a science-driven industry that requires large up-front investment.

Because scientific leaders typically have extensive academic training, they are typically used to focusing on scientific matters more than on business. Their performance has generally been measured on funding, publications, and patents. Their time frames are generally long term, and their work is painstakingly precise, peer reviewed, and extremely specialized (Angermuller, 2017). Although research scientists are well paid, they are typically not paid enormous amounts of money, like engineers. They tend to value status and credit more than engineers do (Angermuller, 2017; Bonawandt & Manganello, 2019; Dodge, 2020). For example, the differences between an associate professor and a full professor or first author and second author may be very important to them. In other words, researchers tend to be more hierarchical than engineers. Job titles and number of publications differentiate faculty and researchers (Angermuller, 2017). Also, even though some research is conducted in teams, the infrastructure supports individual achievement more than teamwork. If researchers work in industry (as opposed to academia, government, or the nonprofit realm), they may value money as well as individual status and credit and may have a lot of work to do to shift into being a team player.

Applied Life Sciences: Pharma, Biotech, and Medical Devices

The fast-growing applied science sector of biological or life sciences includes pharmaceuticals, biotech, and medical device development. These disciplines rely on science to develop medical treatments, devices, and drug (also called "therapeutic") products. It takes enormous effort to discover therapeutics that not only work but are safe. For example, the median investment to bring a new U.S. Food and Drug Administration (FDA)-approved drug to market approximated $2 billion in 2019, and the average drug takes over 12 years to develop (Steedman et al., 2020; Wouters et al., 2020). Huge investments are made, and fundraising is a critical part of this industry. Because these products take so long to get to market, productivity is typically measured by the rate of spending of the venture capital investment (called "burn rate") instead of profit. It is generally a very slow-moving process. A drug development project—and even an entire company—can come to a grinding halt in mid swing because of an FDA decision or competitor being first to market. Regulation and competition can be extremely impactful—instantaneously killing product development and whole companies when approvals are not granted—and thus drive scientists to work extremely hard under a lot of stress.

Drug discovery requires highly trained (often doctoral-level) experts in multiple fields to work together. These fields include subspecialties within chemistry, biology, pharmacology, toxicology, clinical testing, physics, engineering, computer science, bioinformatics, mathematics, statistics, and so on (Geoui, 2016). Individuals are so specialized they often work on teams with people whose training is in a range of specializations. They also work with people in different functions and stages in the drug discovery and development processes, including regulatory, marketing, legal, and manufacturing. Teamwork and collaboration are critical and often the source of much conflict and miscommunication. Scientific and academic leaders not infrequently are the product of academic environments in which individual achievement is paramount; translating that to industry is the root of many challenges in this industry.

Although scientists in this industry are generally motivated by science at the core, many move out of academia because they can make more money elsewhere (Madhusoodanan, 2014). Some may want to strike it rich at a start-up, while others go to big pharma companies to have stable jobs. Some may be motivated by helping to save and improve the lives of people rather than conducting research for the sake of knowledge. Leaders in this industry are typically older than engineers because they have to get so much more training to enter it. They may have more maturity, but the underlying effects of dysfunctional leadership are no less present.

Health Care

The health care industry has been under considerable turmoil for some time, as our society grapples with how best to administer and pay for it. Increasingly, competition among providers and increased technological innovation offer new ways to provide patient care. And then, there is the recent worldwide pandemic. Despite being an industry that remained relatively stable for decades, health care increasingly has had to respond to demands for rapid change (Balser, 2019; Loria, 2019). Health care leaders who have resisted change, in particular, have faced demands that they be replaced with executives from outside of the industry who are more business and customer focused (Loria, 2019).

Like other scientists, medical doctors tend to be very smart, independent thinkers who, by their training and orientation, are focused more on individual achievement and less on teamwork (Balser, 2019; Lamb et al., 2018; Stoller et al., 2016). Modern health care is structured around teamwork, however, and some medical schools are training residents on what they call interprofessional education to prepare them for working in physician-led health care teams and prioritizing the team's needs over their own (American Medical Association, 2014). Unlike scientists, practicing physicians interact directly with patients and are expected to have high levels of people skills and compassion. Also, unlike scientists and more like engineers, they have to solve problems on the basis of existing knowledge, rather than exploring for knowledge's sake. However, medical doctors often straddle the fence between science and practice, just as many organizational consultants do. Many physicians are affiliated with universities, and they teach and conduct research in addition to seeing patients. Their professional organizations are highly regulated, and they must deal with enormous amounts of bureaucracy because of insurance companies. Physician compensation is going down while the amount of work—especially unpleasant administrative work, such as navigating regulations, authorizations, and electronic records—is going up; burnout is a significant concern for people in this field (Dagi, 2017; Lagasse, 2021; Walker, 2019). In one study of more than 3,500 second-year resident physicians, for example, 45.2% reported symptoms of burnout, and 14.1% reported career choice regret (Dyrbye et al., 2018).

Much of consulting to health care providers focuses on business strategy. Psychologists tend to help more in supporting HR with talent management and learning and development. They are also sometimes brought in as coaches to help physicians and other leaders with management and people skills (Balser, 2019; Rathmell et al., 2019). Practitioners, such as physicians and nurses, are increasingly being trained in empathy and "bedside manner" because of recent downward trends in these areas (Litman, 2018). Organizational consultants and HR specialists are being employed to work on these programs.

Engineering: High Tech, Software Development, Building, and Manufacturing

Unlike science and health care, engineering processes—especially software development—tend to move forward at lightning speed. Logistically, software is easy to write and modify; it does not depend on any materials or living organisms except the coders. Hardware, building, and manufacturing are not quite as nimble, but they still tend to operate on much shorter timeframes than scientific research does. In fact, Agile, the dominant tech development methodology, was created to be fast and flexible (Beck et al., 2001).

Engineering development is also faster than development in medical industries because government regulatory agencies generally do not drive the pace of innovation. In computing applications, compatibility is an important issue (e.g., with different operating systems, security, or internet protocols), but it is generally resolved by internal testing, not by external supervision. Government compliance is important for safety and security, especially for applications that convey customer and patient data. Structural engineering and manufacturing have more government supervision, typically for safety reasons. Compliance is likely to become more of an issue in the future as we become increasingly dependent on automation, information, and technology. To date, however, the tech industry has generally shown great resistance to government pressure.

Another distinctive characteristic of engineering is that, although engineers tend to be very intelligent, it is not necessary to be as highly educated as in some of the other tech fields. It is a very applied field, so graduate training in research is generally not helpful. Engineers tend to be motivated by money, and they tend to be paid very well (Bonawandt & Manganello, 2019; Dodge, 2020). Some get very wealthy at noticeably young ages. For example, 22% of the billionaires on Forbes' 2020 list of the 100 richest people in the world were engineers, and many of them became millionaires before they turned 30 (Forbes, 2020). Most engineers are not billionaires, but many are offered large signing bonuses, often right out of college (Leadem, 2017). The lack of maturity of these wealthy young engineers has muddied the reputation of the tech industry and has created terrible role models for tech leaders in general (Epstein & Shelton, 2019; Solon, 2017). Engineers, however, tend to be motivated by solving problems, and they tend to work very hard whether or not they have accumulated wealth.

TECHNICAL LEADERS ARE DIFFERENT FROM NONTECHNICAL LEADERS

When I talk to people about the uniqueness of technical leaders, some instantly know what I mean, and others wonder whether technical leaders really are different from nontechnical leaders. Research shows that technical leaders tend to share certain characteristics, but the question still comes up as to why. Is it because these fields tend to attract people with certain personality traits, abilities, or interests, or is it because the individuals are positively reinforced for behaving in certain ways? Could it be because of the particular challenges they face with the technical teams they lead? Even though some generalizations can be made, it is important to remember that individual leaders may vary a great deal and may not fit these descriptions.

Technical leaders tend to be very bright, curious, analytical, independent thinkers, and the worlds of STEM in which they work, as discussed, are often extraordinarily complex (Emison, 2011; Rounds et al., 2021; Sato, 2016; Wai et al., 2009). Technical leaders tend to be scientists at their core (Hurd, 2009), meaning that they trained as scientists, engineers, and/or in other technical fields, and that is a fundamental part of their identity. They tend to be focused, often linear thinkers who sweat the details, sometimes focusing less on the big picture. The lack of big-picture thinking can frustrate nontechnical businesspeople because they seem to be less concerned with the future of the company and more focused on addressing the technical details. For their part, technical leaders would argue that the technical details are critical for the future. For example, during the COVID-19 crisis, scientists were concerned about safety and spread of the disease, whereas business leaders were concerned with keeping their companies operational. Neither was "right" or "wrong," but often they presented themselves and their views that way (Stankiewicz, 2020).

Consistent with the nature of their work, technical leaders tend to be data-driven, rational thinkers who make decisions logically, supported by data and facts, as they were trained to do in math, science, and engineering classes in school (Chen & Simpson, 2015; Daniels, 2009; Glass, 2006; Kumar & Hsiao, 2007; Rathmell et al., 2019; Sansone & Schreiber-Abshire, 2011). They often seem not to want emotions to cloud their judgment. For example, a technical leader mused during a career conversation about how long he should stay with his current company. He had worked up a spreadsheet with all the variables and had conducted several calculations to make this decision, but he was not certain about the "right" answer. When asked how he felt about it, he said that his feelings about it did not matter. It had to be a rational decision.

Throughout their careers, technical leaders are generally reinforced for being right, not wrong. A circuit works or it doesn't; code has a bug or it doesn't; medicine cures or it doesn't. When technical leaders disagree, they may defend their positions adamantly, leading to heated debates and even to insubordination. They also tend to be independent thinkers, which may affect attempts to collaborate within and across teams.

The lack of feelings associated with rational thinking can present as a lack of empathy for others (Jack et al., 2013). This topic often arises when coaching technical leaders, according to interviews with consultants I conducted for this book. For example, Debbie Rocco, one of the interviewees, has led in-house learning and development programs in the high-tech, biotech, and health care industries, and she has worked as a talent management consultant in organizations all over the world. She reported how she observed that scientists and engineers differed from leaders in other industries:

> In my experience working with technical leaders in telecommunications or biotechnology, they are trained to be good independent thinkers. Their success is based on how good they were as a technical individual contributor. This is true of all leaders, but particularly true for technical leaders—it is a very different skill set that makes a good leader, and they have to move from getting their satisfaction from being a doer to getting their work done through others. (D. Rocco, personal communication, April 13, 2020)

Technical leaders' personal characteristics can create challenges because of the people and products they have to oversee. Technical people, by both their nature and their training, tend to be skeptical. They are taught to question everything all the time, and people with this style of communication can be challenging to lead. They are also highly concerned with risk mitigation because failure in their work can have catastrophic consequences (Glass, 2006). Their skepticism can cause them to be less open to outsiders, such as organizational consultants, and to the instruments and methods consultants use. For example, one HR leader in the Bay Area told me about how the developers in a few different very famous organizations she has worked in "won't give outside consultants the time of day." She observed that they trusted HR more, but she admitted that she still found it challenging to break through their skepticism from that role too.

There are, of course, exceptions to these generalizations. Some technical leaders are more people oriented and focused on the big picture than others. These are often the technical leaders who are successful in dealing with people outside of their departments. Additionally, some technical leaders are highly creative and tend to be less unilaterally rationally driven, with greater access to nonlinear thinking. They may be just as independent and challenged to collaborate with others, and they may create conflict on the team (Nemeth et al., 2004; Petrou et al., 2020).

As organizational consultants well know, there is no secret formula for successful leadership. Because each person is distinctive, a single approach will not work for everyone. This is true of technical people, too. Nick Armstrong, whom I interviewed for this book, is a marketing consultant, web designer, and TEDx speaker who has worked with many tech entrepreneurs. He observed, "It's possible to be a geeky introvert who is a good leader, and it's possible to be an extroverted people-person who is a bad leader" (N. Armstrong, personal communication, April 2, 2020).

Leadership Challenges for Technical Leaders

Technical leaders can struggle to gain credibility because they may have limited business acumen and people skills. They tend to focus on the necessary minutia of new product creation and not always focus on the big picture when it comes to running a company. They are therefore not always taken seriously as business leaders and may have difficulty influencing people outside of their own technical organization. Technical leaders have not traditionally been at the executive table, and it may be a change for everyone to invite them there. For example, one global study of more than 1,400 top-level technical and business leaders showed that, even though they all said that technology was critical to business success, technical leaders were limited in their influence because others did not see them as business leaders. Deloitte's 2018 global chief information officer survey results indicated that IT leaders still felt like they were perceived by other leaders as "order takers," not business drivers (Briggs et al., 2018). In other Deloitte studies, only 29% of business leaders agreed that the technology organization and its leaders should be deeply involved in developing enterprise business strategy, while technical leaders reported that they needed to be involved in business decisions (Kark et al., 2019, 2020).

For their part, technical leaders have often done relatively little to develop their leadership skills. Too often, they do not keep up with leaders in other industries in self-development efforts. The large-scale Deloitte study of more than 25,000 leaders identified four areas in which leadership development for technical leaders fell behind that of other industries (DDI et al., 2018). First, compared with leaders in other industries, technical leaders reported less often that they had a clear understanding of their career path. In addition, technical organizations reported lower engagement and higher turnover than other industries did. Second, the majority of technical leaders reported that they did not have individual development plans, suggesting they had little accountability for improving their leadership. Third, technical leaders reported a higher reliance on internal coaching and self-study than did other leaders, and that was incongruent with the more formal kinds of development that the leaders wanted. Fourth, technical leaders more often reported that they had never met with their manager to talk about performance or development than did leaders in other industries.

This study also looked at what types of leadership development opportunities technical leaders wanted. The top three leadership development methods they identified were (a) external coaching, (b) formal leadership development, and (c) short-term leadership development assignments

(DDI et al., 2018). Unfortunately, the study found that tech companies provided these three types of leadership development least often, compared to companies in other industries. Of the technical leaders, 74% indicated they wanted to have external coaching, 60% wanted formal development, and 50% wanted short-term developmental assignments. These development methods were offered least often compared with other industries.

Another common challenge for technical leaders is that leadership roles tend to be ambiguous. For example, matrix-based structures are frequently employed, in which employees report to multiple supervisors, perhaps in an informal or dotted-line way. The employees work in multiple teams and have a formal reporting structure for organizational reasons, yet the manager may not know what they are working on. Matrix structures often provide team leaders and managers with little or undefined formal authority. Employees may have titles such as chief engineer, project owner, lead program manager, or senior project manager; these job descriptions and performance expectations vary widely, as do the roles and responsibilities, between functions and organizations (Vieth & Smith, 2008). This uncertainty can lead individuals to feel disempowered when they are managing people (BlessingWhite, 2013). Also, given the little training offered, some technical leaders stumble when they take on their first management position, and that can cut into their confidence as a leader.

Costs of Not Developing Technical Leaders

Without substantial motivation to change or training on how, people tend to resort to what they know and stick with what makes them comfortable (Crosby, 2021). For technical leaders, that is the technology. Without direction, they often tend either to dive back into the technical role of "doing" instead of "managing," leaving the team stranded, or to stay so engaged in the details that the team feels micromanaged. Organizations lose out when technical leaders are ineffective. Innovation, decision making, problem solving, communication, and engagement suffer, and, most important, team members do not have the opportunity to contribute their best thinking, which is critical to technical teams: "An unprepared second-level manager becomes a significant bottleneck in the system. Such individuals are unable to function effectively in any direction. And most problematic, they cannot support or be a role model for their first-level managers" (Hurd, 2009, p. 44).

With all these challenges with technical leaders, why not just bring in nontechnical leaders to lead and manage in technical organizations? Research shows that leaders who have domain-specific expertise are more successful than leaders who do not (Markman, 2017). For example, hospitals run by doctors perform better than hospitals run by leaders from different backgrounds (Stoller et al., 2016). When their leader is technically competent in their domain of expertise, employees are happier, more productive, and leave less frequently (Artz et al., 2016). This finding suggests that it may be better to train technical people in how to lead rather than to rely on nontechnical people for leadership roles. It is generally quicker and easier to train technical people in leadership skills on the job than to teach nontechnical leaders technical skills that often take years of education to master (Felder et al., 2016).

IMPLICATIONS FOR ORGANIZATIONAL CONSULTANTS

Even though technical and other industries have distinct differences, they are, in many ways, just organizations filled with people. Organizational consultants can often make headway consulting to technical leaders by using standard organizational consulting practices (American Psychological Association, 2017; Lowman, 2016). However, there is more work to be done, because, as previously noted, technical industries lag behind other industries in leadership development. Understanding industry contexts and tweaking consulting practices can help. More specifically, the methods described in this book are about tailoring the amount and level of information about the consulting process provided to clients rather than changing existing evidence-based consulting practices, though new practices are expected to emerge over time and with new technology (as described in Chapter 7).

Organizational Consultants Need to Adapt
Their Approach for Technical Leaders

Research conducted by many large consulting firms (e.g., Deloitte, EY, DDI, and GP Strategies, with companies in varying industries across the globe) suggests that people who specialize in learning and development (L&D) tend not to communicate in a way that resonates with technical leaders, and they do not necessarily understand their priorities either. For example, BlessingWhite, a subsidiary of the large global technical training company GP Strategies, surveyed technical and HR leaders in more than 300 organizations (BlessingWhite, 2013). The researchers asked technical leaders and L&D leaders to identify the top leadership challenges for technical leaders. The two groups of leaders had different answers. Whereas technical leaders ranked "delivering on projects with fewer resources" as their top challenge, L&D leaders ranked "developing myself both personally and professionally" as the technical leaders' top challenge. In general, the findings showed that the technical leaders were primarily focused on delivering project results and making sure the team had the technical expertise to do so, and the L&D leaders were primarily concerned with the people and team dynamics on the technical teams.

Other large consulting firms report similar findings (DDI et al., 2018). In short, technical leaders perceive that HR leadership development efforts do not meet their needs. Technical leaders may perceive that development efforts are too generic because high-level nontechnical executives do not understand their unique needs. Most important, they find that HR and L&D do not adequately communicate the value of their services using metrics that technical and business leaders appreciate. Whether these are blind spots for L&D because they do not understand the needs of technical leaders or they are blind spots for technical leaders themselves does not really matter. The disconnect is there. The question is, how can organizational consultants break through that?

Some evidence suggests that the context is slowly changing, and more technical leaders are warming up to the idea of developing their so-called soft skills. Rebecca Johannsen, an educator and consultant in the area of emotional intelligence, observed during my interview with her that "in over

10 years of consulting in this area, I've seen an evolution in the understanding that the interpersonal skills are needed. I have to make less of a case for it now than I used to for technical leaders" (R. Johannsen, personal communication, April 6, 2020).

The competition for talent has forced fast-growing technical industries to change their approach. The Silicon Valley tech industry is one example: "Twenty years ago, management skills were neither taught nor rewarded in Silicon Valley, but today its companies are *obsessed* with it" (Scott, 2019, p. xxvii). When there is an abundance of jobs to choose from, people quit if they do not like their bosses. In fact, feeling that one has a bad manager is one of the top reasons people quit companies (Reina et al., 2017). Not all STEM industries and geographical locations have the luxury of an abundance of jobs, however, and some technical people have never experienced a better way to work than in a trying, unsupportive environment.

Even when there is the motive to work on leadership development, organizational consultants still face the barrier that there is little to no time to develop. Sean Ristine, VP of HR in a biotech company, told me that it is a resource and time issue:

> They are so invested in the work of the moment and are not looking forward. It's HR's responsibility to develop forward thinking. We get a lot of upper management pushback. They say, "We don't have time for that right now." Then a tech expert gets promoted and is not equipped, and they have to play catch up. (S. Ristine, personal communication, July 17, 2020)

Consulting to Technical Leaders Is More About Nuance Than a Fundamental Shift

Sometimes when I tell people, including other consultants, that I consult to technical leaders they ask me whether they are really any different from other leaders. After all, organizational leadership theories tend to be industry independent (Landis et al., 2014). Is it necessary to create a new theory specifically for technical leaders?

Developing new leadership theories to describe technical leadership does not seem necessary because existing leadership theories of situational, trait, and competency-based leadership can be applied to technical contexts (Landis et al., 2014). Situational leadership theory, for example, can be interpreted as taking the industry into consideration because "any particular situation plays a large part in determining leadership qualities and the leader for that situation" (Bass, 1990, p. 39). Trait- and competency-based theories of leadership can explain leadership success and failure in technical industries to the extent that people with certain traits are attracted to and/or are successful in technical occupations and these traits coincide with or conflict with leadership traits and competencies, including technical competencies (Derue et al., 2011). This idea is explored in more detail in Chapter 4.

Rather than suggesting new theories specific to the technical context, this book focuses on the nuances of situations that tend to occur in technical organizations and on the typical characteristics of the individuals who tend to work in technical leadership positions. It is intended to guide consultants who consult with or aim to consult with technical leaders about characteristics of technical employees and their organizational cultures, specific challenges technical leaders face in their organizations, and what their development needs are. Throughout the book, I illustrate the major concepts with information and quotations from a variety of technical leaders and consultants I interviewed. I aim to prepare organizational consultants to deal with the challenges they may to run into when consulting with technical leaders. I describe contexts in which leaders in the STEM fields are working to help consultants to understand what to learn to be confident and credible with technical clients. I also provide tools to employ in consulting at the individual, group, and organizational levels in technical organizations and outline potential future directions in STEM industries and in consulting to technical leaders for consultants to conduct research and further their consulting skills.

2

Understanding Technical Leaders: What Challenges Are They Facing?

I have found one of the key differentiators between organizational consultants who thrive in consulting with technical leaders and ones who suffer through or avoid it is whether they truly understand and embrace the context of the technical leaders. Beyond simply understanding the work context, consultants who are successful with this type of leadership consultation understand, appreciate, and adapt to the scientific mindset of technical people.

One of the conclusions in Chapter 1 was that there seems to be misalignment between what technical leaders' priorities are and what organizational consultants and learning and development (L&D) leaders think they should be, especially in terms of leadership development. Because the survey research was limited in the richness of detail it provided, I decided to collect qualitative data in the form of interviews with technical leaders, organizational consultants, and human resources (HR) leaders.

https://doi.org/10.1037/0000270-003
Consulting to Technical Leaders, Teams, and Organizations: Building Leadership in STEM Environments, by J. B. Connell

I asked open-ended questions to hear their experiences in their own words. This chapter presents highlights and direct quotes from the interviews to paint a detailed picture of what technical leaders are facing as well as how organizational consultants and HR leaders experience working with them.

INTERVIEW STUDY OF TECHNICAL LEADERS, ORGANIZATIONAL CONSULTANTS, AND HR LEADERS

I interviewed a total of 60 leaders: 25 technical leaders, 25 organizational consultants, and 10 HR leaders, all of whom worked with technical leaders or organizations. The interviews were part of a qualitative research study (Bengtsson, 2016; Levitt, 2019). Participants were recruited primarily through email and LinkedIn campaigns that targeted a diverse array of people in the three different domains of technical leaders in science, technology, engineering, and mathematics (STEM), consultants who worked with technical leaders, and HR leaders who worked with technical leaders. Participants and those who made referrals were offered entrance into a lottery for Amazon gift cards. Semistructured interviews lasted 30 minutes and were conducted by telephone using an interview guide consisting of 15 questions. Responses were content analyzed by a team of psychology researchers, and the themes are presented in the next sections, along with quotes from the participants. All interviewees consented to have their data and quotations from their interviews included in this book either by name or anonymously.

Do Technical Organizations Need to Have Technical Leaders?

Regardless of whether organizational consultants think that technical leaders need to have technical backgrounds, they need to understand that technical leaders believe that to be the case. Over 90% of the technical leaders I interviewed said that technical organizations need to have technically trained leaders. In fact, most were quite emphatic. Larry Heminger, chief technology officer (CTO) of a computing firm, put it succinctly: "People wouldn't have it any other way" (L. Heminger, personal communication, April 24, 2020).

Several major explanations were given as to why technical leaders thought they needed to have technical backgrounds. Quoted excerpts from the interviews are in italics, followed by brief descriptions of the technical leaders to understand their context.

- **To build credibility among technical teams.** *You need the respect of the team. More often than not, that comes from having experience and having empathy for developers* (E. de Bruin, personal communication, April 21, 2020). Etienne de Bruin leads the global CTO community called 7CTOs.

- **To understand the technology and development process.** *Leadership is creating an environment where people can feel safe, comfortable, and they can trust someone when they have questions or need direction* (J. Molina, personal communication, April 29, 2020). Joe Molina is the executive director of the National Veterans Chamber of Commerce.

- **To advocate for technical teams.** *Technical leaders need to be technical because there's so much nuanced understanding that comes from the engineering backgrounds* (M. Shirman, personal communication, April 29, 2020). Misha Shirman is a CTO of an early-stage bioinformatics and data company.

- **To support technical teams.** *Technical teams need to know that their leader has their backs. Senior management frequently consists of people with primarily venture investment or financial backgrounds. There is always pressure from these . . . people who do not understand the required processes, [and] the complex challenges and typical execution times, especially with outsourcing. The technical team needs a technical leader to advocate for them. The nontechnical person may not have the respect of the other senior management members or the ability to explain things to them to help them understand why the team needs the support. Therefore, the technical leader needs to educate and inform other executives which really needs to be part of the technical leader's job description* (G. Stetsko, personal communication, October 23, 2020). Gina Stetsko has been a vice president of pharmaceutical development and operations in multiple pharmaceutical start-ups.

- **To assess compliance risk.** *It's understanding the risk involved in a certain level of decisions. A company needs to execute in a way that is compliant with laws for data security and that doesn't open infrastructure to security issues* (V. Baranov, personal communication, April 27, 2020). Vladimir Baranov is the CTO of a midsize fintech (i.e., financial technology) company.

- **To stay focused.** *The CEO of a small SaaS [software as a service] business was the archetype arsonist—one who has the ever-changing chaotic mindset of an entrepreneurial CEO, like an arsonist setting fires everywhere. He was at the far end of entrepreneurial spirit. He burned out and frustrated his technical team week in and week out. There was so much discord because of his changing priorities* (M. Valenzano, personal communication, April 17, 2020). Michael Valenzano consults with organizations to create effective company cultures.

- **To evaluate time and resources.** *In one organization I worked with, there was not a common language for the CFO [chief financial officer] and the tech teams to speak. They had trouble setting expectations. The technical talent did not have sufficient leadership skills to help their manager (the CFO) understand how to manage them well. The CFO wasn't willing or able to make the right accommodations to meet the technical folks where they were at to develop them. The CFO expected them to take the orders directly . . . The [CFO-to-developer relationship] didn't work because it was too much of a gap* (S. Krawitz, personal communication, April 7, 2020). Scott Krawitz is a seasoned tech leader and former CTO who has worked in many different tech-enabled companies.

- **Caveat: It depends on where the leadership is.** *We have a VP of engineering who did not come from a technical background. She's been phenomenal at the team aspect and has picked up the technology she needs. She has some support from the technical folks, like myself and other senior people on the team. You can have a technical team led by someone who's nontechnical, but they need to have some level of support. The amount depends on where they are. On a day-to-day level, I spend zero time on engineering issues. I focus on architecture* (M. Karia, personal communication, April 10, 2020). Meetesh Karia is CTO of The Zebra, an Austin-based tech company known for successfully hiring and promoting people from diverse and nontraditional backgrounds.

- **To increase employee satisfaction.** *If your boss understands the nature of the work, then they can actually help you. They can assess you well, and they can encourage you in the right direction to advance in your career, and that is a very important element for job satisfaction* (A. Goodall, in an interview on the *HBR IdeaCast*, as cited in Carmichael, 2018). Amanda Goodall, senior lecturer at Cass Business School of the City University of London, was speaking of her findings from her research on hospitals and other organizations.

In summary, the sample of technical leaders tended to give situational reasons for why technical organizations and teams needed technical leaders; the reasons focused primarily on the importance of having the competency to understand the technical aspects of the technology, business, and work.

Leaders in tech often used the word "empathy" to describe understanding the practical context, or work environment, of their employees rather than the emotions they experience, and they seemed to believe overarchingly that the only way to have this sort of empathy is to have training and experience in technical work. Personality fit with the technical work environment may be a factor too (Nauta, 2010; Rounds et al., 2021). Understanding context was a major misalignment between technical leaders and organizational consultants, as found in the survey research described in Chapter 1 (DDI, 2018). The next section focuses on the details of the technical leaders' context, to help organizational consultants better align with them.

What Are the Technical Leaders' Priorities and Challenges?

When I asked technical leaders about their "big-picture" concerns, several themes emerged. These focused on talent, rapid change, balancing technology with business, communicating, and project management. Technical leaders seemed to face similar daily challenges overall. They reported their daily leadership challenges primarily consisted of communicating, managing, motivating and supporting their team, delegating, and managing work expectations. Following are examples of what they said:

- **Hiring and keeping talent.** *The average tenure of the developer is pretty short. There is always a fear of where the next tech talent will come from. Keeping talent is also critical* (S. Sundukovskiy, personal communication, April 24, 2020). Sergey Sundukovskiy is the CTO of a small tech company. He stood out from other CTOs because he has a doctorate in organization and management.

- **Keeping up with rapid change.** *Things are changing at too rapid a pace to keep up in technology work. It's a struggle from both a company and a business perspective. We have financial companies and technology companies as competition. You have to be ahead of the curve, and that's really hard to do* (S. Moran, personal communication, April 14, 2020). Sarah Moran is the former head of innovation in a large multinational fintech company.

- **Balancing customer and business concerns.** *The challenge is finding a balance between creating new tech capabilities and features and managing technical debt* (K. van der Raadt, personal communication, May 7, 2020). Krijn van der Raadt is the senior director of software engineering at AppFolio.

- **Communicating to teams and across the organization.** *My current role is in upper middle management. I am not in the C-Suite, but I am bridging the gap between the high-level vision and the people who execute* (K. van der Raadt, personal communication, May 7, 2020).

- **Managing projects and problems.** *My top daily challenges are keeping staff informed, making sure everything is done, paperwork is done, solving problems, making sure problems are solved, and sales* (B. Salomon, personal communication, April 3, 2020). Bob Salomon is the CEO of CIO Systems, a small IT service firm.

- **Motivating and managing the team.** *[My daily leadership challenges center on] how to constructively motivate people to treat the project or client as if it were their own, finding time to support the team, and not seeming annoyed. Also being the tie breaker for all conflicts or differences* *of opinion and being the sole person responsible for accuracy of all work products* (D. Wallace, personal communication, April 9, 2020). David Wallace is the CEO of a small construction business in the renewables and environment industry.

- **Delegating and managing work expectations.** *One of my big challenges is holding people accountable, especially other leaders and leaders at higher levels* (C. Jessen, personal communication, June 8, 2020). Chan Jessen is a leader in a large construction company.

The challenges may not be all that different from those experienced by leaders of any sort of team, but there were some further insights from the consultants and HR leaders. When I asked the sample of organizational consultants who worked with technical companies to identify the big-picture issues on which they saw technical leaders focusing, many of them said technical leaders lacked visionary thinking. The leaders may have been focused on future technology challenges, but business strategy tended not to be part of their thinking. The consultants agreed with the technical leaders, however, that communication was a top concern for them. Following are some examples of how they described the technical leaders' challenges with the big picture:

- **Collaborating for big-picture results.** *From what I have experienced, the bridge between the research and development teams is difficult to build and requires a lot of collaboration. Sometimes the difficulties come from lack of collaboration or not taking the time to think about downstream systems and processes. It is common for preclinical teams to be so focused on the early research that they are not preparing for selecting materials and processes that are scalable. That presents a challenge to the later-stage development teams* (personal communication by an individual who did not wish to be cited by name, May 5, 2020).
- **Balancing short- and long-term thinking.** *Based on when I was working with technical leaders, I saw there was a lot of pressure to be able to think short term and long term and to balance those. From a business perspective, they have to move fast, respond to customers, and deal with rapid change. There's a need to get the infrastructure and ability to do*

that, but they also have to think about the infrastructure for the future. Where is the ball going? How will I meet a set of needs that haven't been articulated yet? (I. Kristic, personal communication, May 7, 2020). Ian Kristic is a senior solutions consultant and regional head at The Myers-Briggs Company.

Another insight was how challenged the technical leaders were in managing emotions, especially frustration, both in the moment and over the long term.

- **Managing in-the-moment frustration.** *I've had challenges with people in our IT department. They get frustrated when clients aren't able to do basic things. For example, one of my team members sent a request to IT. She thought she had an IT problem, but it was really an issue of how to upload a program to Excel. I thought the IT guy was going to explode because it was such a simple problem* (personal communication by an individual who did not wish to be cited by name, April 30, 2020).

- **Managing ongoing frustration.** *There is a buildup of frustration and anxiety from the beginning. Nobody has ever told them the solution to a sociotechnical problem is much different from the solution to a technical problem. With a technical problem, there is generally a right or at least reasonable answer. With a management problem, there is no right and perhaps no decent answer. Technical people often think if they give you more facts, figures, or calculations, they'll convert you to their way of thinking. I've seen a lot of potential leaders get out of it before they give it a good shot. They quit because there is little to no effective mentoring to indicate how to deal with people issues. They're not willing to put in the effort, to develop the skill set needed. We lose some really good people out of university administration and industrial management because of that* (D. Hess, personal communication, July 10, 2020). Throughout his career, Dr. Dennis Hess (professor emeritus in the School of Chemical & Biomolecular Engineering at the Georgia Institute of Technology and author of *Leadership by Engineers and Scientists: Professional Skills Needed To Succeed in a Changing World*) observed a high level of frustration among technical leaders in STEM, in academic settings as well as in industry.

Overall, technical leaders and organizational consultants and HR leaders seemed to observe similar priorities and challenges in technical leaders' work. The difference was in how they expressed and emphasized them. Consistent with the research described in Chapter 1, the technical leaders seemed to focus more on the results, and the consultants and HR leaders focused more on the process. This difference might help to explain why they are not speaking the same language. Later chapters in this book focus on techniques for organizational consultants to use to better align with technical leaders. Before proceeding to that point, however, it may be worthwhile to understand how technical leaders have developed their leadership skills and what they think they could improve.

What Leadership Skills Do Technical Leaders Think They Need to Develop?

The technical leaders, organizational consultants, and HR leaders who were interviewed generally agreed that the top skills technical leaders need to develop were (a) interpersonal skills in terms of emotional intelligence and empathy; (b) communication skills, especially cross-functional communication, listening, and collaborating; and (c) developing the team, such as coaching and motivating team members and building trust in the team. Other important skills were learning to let go and delegate work, managing conflict, and influencing. The leaders and consultants gave a variety of reasons, as follows:

- **Emotional intelligence.** *The average tech person is brain first, emotion second, if it's even that high on the list* (D. Wallace, personal communication, April 9, 2020).
- **Communication skills.** *It takes a lot of effort to communicate clearly. Sometimes I'm lazy and don't communicate well and have to spend more time on the back end explaining myself. When I do invest up front and put in the energy to be clear, I get a better result* (R. Yumul, personal communication, May 6, 2020). Rich Yumul is the CEO of Sage Tree Solutions, a digital marketing and web application firm.

- **Managing the fast pace.** *There are so many moving parts, I need to provide quick feedback to close the loops. It comes down to bridging strategic and tactical in a way that's effective and timely. I'm bridging different operating levels* (K. van der Raadt, personal communication, May 7, 2020).

- **Developing the team.** *If you want to motivate people, you don't need to know everything technical better than everyone else. You need to create an environment where people feel that they are heard, that is more hospitable, not focused only on data. Early in my career, I thought it was important to be the smartest person in the room, and I thought that was what drove success. Eventually, I found that adjusting to the needs of the people in the room built a more open, accepting, safe environment that allowed for the best ideas to be offered up. This also promoted interpersonal communication and understanding within the team. In one organization where I cared more about the people, some cried when I left. That was a sign that I had created the right environment* (G. Stetsko, personal communication, October 23, 2020).

- **Letting go.** *What got me here was being a good problem solver. I need to learn how to step back and always improve on giving my team space or enabling/coaching them to solve problems. I always thought managing people was telling them what to do, but in reality, I have 70 people telling me what to do* (M. Noori, personal communication, April 30, 2020). Manijeh Noori is the VP of engineering at The Zebra.

Several organizational consultants noted that technical leaders would benefit from developing coaching skills so they could guide their team members and empower them at the same time. For example, Mike Nowland, a leadership development consultant who had coached and trained countless technical leaders, observed that technical leaders could fall into two traps when leading others:

> Technical leaders tend to do one of two things. Either they go for what I call "delegation by abdication," as in "this is yours, go do it," assuming it would be done as they would do it. Then if the person needs help, because it's so easy in the leader's brain, they can't break it down for them, and they both get frustrated. Or they take the opposite approach

and do not delegate enough as they know how to do it all. So, they micromanage their direct reports leaving them frustrated and wondering why "he's getting all up in my stuff and micromanaging me." (M. Nowland, personal communication, April 3, 2020)

Hurd's (2009) research on technical leaders, whom she collectively called *scientists*, corroborates Nowland's observations. Hurd's research revealed that scientists were challenged by having to let go of their personal active involvement in the science as they moved into management; being a scientist was core to their identity. Delegating and empowering others could be the most challenging, in part because it meant letting go of the details of the science. Collaborating was often a challenge too, especially for scientists who started their careers in academia where they were rewarded for their own ideas. Caring about what happened to other departments in the organization may have been new to them as well because academic departments tend to be siloed. Managing people was a whole new set of skills for scientists because it was not included in their training or necessarily modeled well in postdocs or in their jobs in industry; rather, they were trained to be technical experts. Influencing others to do things rather than dictating the right course of action could be a challenge for scientists who are used to scientifically proven answers and ways of doing things. Being able to deliver and receive honest feedback were skills that generally needed development among scientists.

How Technical Leaders Developed Their Leadership Skills

Most leaders in the interview study reported developing their leadership skills by trial and error on the job; through books, podcasts, and other self-taught methods; or through aspects of their personal lives, such as becoming a parent, participating in therapy, playing team sports, or leading clubs. Some leaders had participated in leadership training programs, either inside or outside of the company, and some had taken university courses in psychology or business. Less than a third of the leaders had been mentored at work by their managers or other colleagues or had received professional coaching or some form of group coaching.

One software leader compared being a team leader to learning parenting skills. They explained, "When the kids were young, it was like managing the team. You had to be very clear about expectations, follow up, and be patient. I learned a lot of interaction skills being a parent." Some leaders said they learned by observing what to do and what not to do from managers along the way. A leader in pharma said, "I never had a mentor. I had nobody. Some of the people I worked for were counterproductive—in fact, almost across the board." Those who learned from good managers felt fortunate to have had that experience.

Some organizational consultants have reported that the amount of leadership development technical leaders get depends on the size of the company. The largest companies tend not only to offer but to encourage or require leadership training. Smaller companies, on the other hand, do not. Rebecca Johannsen told her story of conducting leadership training in two contrasting organizations, a large one and a small one:

> I worked with two organizations that were vastly different. One gave lots of time off to develop soft skills. The organization prioritized this. The same week, I went to deliver a program to another organization that wanted too much information crammed into 2 hours with too many people in the room. They wanted me to help them make more of a priority of soft skills in hiring. One company had an extensive leadership development program for their technical leaders. The people in the room with me had participated in several of these programs. The company had incentivized them to participate because they recognized the need. We had smaller numbers of people (10) to work on material in depth. Organizations that say "it's nice to have" cram as many people in the room and limit it to two hours. (R. Johannsen, personal communication, April 6, 2020)

Tracy Ward is an HR consultant and founder of Forward Talent Strategies, and she previously held an executive leadership role as VP of corporate culture. In her experience with technical industries, she has found that

> companies differ in how much investment they put into different positions and training. Sometimes they have forums for employees'

own personal development. They might provide investment in a mastermind group or provide individual coaching for an employee. It shows great investment in the employee and supports their success rather than leaving them to figure things out on their own. Their own leader is also hugely impactful in their development. (T. Ward, personal communication, April 23, 2020)

How Do Technical Leaders Identify and Nurture Potential Leaders?

There was little consensus among the leaders I interviewed regarding how to identify potential leaders. Some said they looked to see if people were already leading in various ways. They tried to find those who, in their current roles, were growing, supporting, and leading others. Some leaders identified potential leaders by asking their team members what they wanted and seeing who had goals and interest in leadership. They said people should be motivated to become leaders, and some believed that leadership skill was an innate quality. For example, Wallace said, "It's a certain DNA. It is intrinsic motivation" (D. Wallace, personal communication, April 9, 2020). Some warned that technical leaders put too much weight on technical skills. In his work with veterans, Joe Molina found that

> Many employers on the IT side (or in any other field) want to promote those with the highest level of technical knowledge. Having the highest level of knowledge does not automatically make that employee a leader of a team; they are of course an expert in the field, but not automatically a leader. (J. Molina, personal communication, April 29, 2020)

Larry Heminger simplified it by category: "There are two kinds of promoting in tech companies. Tech to tech is metrics and skills based. Tech to management is different. The skills you need to lead are above and beyond tech skills" (L. Heminger, personal communication, April 24, 2020).

How do the technical leaders nurture potential leaders? Hardly any of the leaders I interviewed reported giving people on their teams opportunities to do leadership training. Rather, it was much less structured.

They talked about giving opportunities with gradually increasing levels of responsibility, sometimes coaching and mentoring along the way, sometimes letting people make mistakes and giving them support after.

Agustin Lebron and Paul Johnson, founding partners of Essilen Research, study and consult to engineering leaders. They have many years of experience leading technical teams in engineering and finance and have been conducting research on engineers since 2014. They said that engineers do three things when hiring that hinder success of the company: "Engineers tend to hire people like they were hired, they hire people like themselves, and they overvalue skills and undervalue raw ability and culture fit" (A. Lebron & P. Johnson, personal communication, September 9, 2020). They said that one reason that engineers default to overvaluing skills is that concrete skills are easy to test, such as skill testing for a particular programming language, and this approach results in interviews that are structured like exams rather than attempts to match individuals to companies.

Lebron and Johnson have found that engineering leaders who are more thoughtful about their hiring process

> blow others away. . . . The difference between a company that uses average hiring practices and one that is great at hiring is like night and day, and the difference in success is remarkable. In fact, survey respondents indicate that great hires are three times more productive on average than average ones, indicating the tremendous value of world-class hiring. (A. Lebron & P. Johnson, personal communication, September 9, 2020)

Other leaders I interviewed talked about the proliferation of technical leaders who really should not be leaders. Typically, these people were excellent technical contributors who were either pressured into becoming leaders against their wishes or thought that was the only path up in the organization and took the promotion even though they had no interest in leading. These leaders were always described as being "miserable to work for." One technical leader who had experience working for a manager who had no interest in managing even went so far as to say, "If you don't want to be a manager, please don't be a manager. It's not [something] you can fake easily."

Camille Fournier (2017) described the *alpha geek* as a prototype to watch out for. The alpha geek's goal is to be the best engineer on the team, to be the smartest person in the room, and to be right at all times. They believe technical competence dictates who makes decisions, they insist on being the central focal point (even taking undue amounts of credit), and they create enough fear on the team to avoid being challenged by others. Even though alpha geeks are not good leaders, they end up in leadership positions all too often. Either managers see them as already leading the team and pressure them to take a leadership role or they feel it is the only path up.

Organizational consultants frequently commented that they saw the best technical people get promoted, not the people with the best leadership and management skills. Some HR leaders reported that technical leaders set a threshold for technical skills that weeds out good potential candidates. They wait until too late in the process to look at leadership skills. Kasey Harboe Guentert had keen observations from her work in developing selection systems in Silicon Valley tech companies:

> The larger tech start-ups have by now mostly developed interview protocols that take into account the right skills, but it's coming later than any other industry. Some have spent many years weeding out excellent candidates because of an excessive emphasis on technical knowledge and skills, and lack of training or confidence in measuring behaviors. (K. Harboe Guentert, personal communication, October 19, 2020)

Organizational consultants can help technical leaders identify individuals with high potential in the workplace and consult to educators and coach technical employees on STEM career paths (Cappelli, 2019; Finkelstein et al., 2018; Ihsan & Furnham, 2018; Johns, 2019; Lamb et al., 2018; Rathmell et al., 2019; Sánchez-Ruiz et al., 2010; Silzer & Church, 2009).

HOW DO CONSULTANTS DEAL WITH
ALL THESE CHALLENGES?

This chapter reports the experiences and perspectives of technical leaders, organizational consultants, and HR leaders on a variety of technical management issues. The remaining chapters in this book identify possible solutions to the issues presented here. The following chapters focus on two things that will increase the success of an organizational consultant or HR leader who is working with technical leaders. The first is helping the consultant overcome commonly encountered barriers to communicating effectively with technical leaders. The second is helping the consultant identify and consult on the needs of technical leaders as described in this chapter.

Chapter 3 focuses on getting the attention of and buy-in, or agreement, from technical leaders to help them solve their people-management challenges. Chapter 4 focuses on consulting at the individual level with technical leaders and helping them develop their leadership skills. Chapter 5 describes context and solutions for consulting at the group level to help technical leaders motivate and manage their teams. Diversity is addressed in this chapter. Chapter 6 describes solutions for working at the organizational level with technical organizations and adding structure, culture, and processes to help technical leaders succeed at cross-functional communication and collaboration. Chapter 7 provides further insight for the challenges that consultants and HR leaders often encounter in ongoing relationships with technical leaders and raises future consulting challenges and opportunities for continued research on technical leaders.

3

Consulting to Technical Leaders: Overcoming Barriers to Entry

To some degree, consulting to technical leaders is like consulting to any kind of leader, but there are also substantial differences. These include certain differences in style, cognition, and values for which it is worth altering or fine tuning one's consulting approach to attain and deliver on projects successfully.

As discussed in Chapter 1, it can be hard to get the interest of technical leaders. Getting a technical leader's attention is similar to getting a busy executive's attention in that a consultant needs to be quick and show immediate value. It is different from getting the busy executive's attention because technical leaders tend to have a much narrower scope of interest— the technical side. A lot of ego may be involved at the executive level and also for technical leaders, but technical leaders' approach can often be accentuated by a more clear-cut, absolute, or black-and-white way of thinking. The idea that technical or scientific questions have a correct answer has

https://doi.org/10.1037/0000270-004
Consulting to Technical Leaders, Teams, and Organizations: Building Leadership in STEM Environments, by J. B. Connell

been hammered in as a way of thinking. Implying to technical leaders that they are wrong in any way may be upsetting. Belle Walker, Silicon Valley engineer turned consultant, has seen a lot of "resentment and fear" when it comes to bringing in consultants (B. Walker, personal communication, July 22, 2020). As she stated in an interview for this book, "There is a culture of overachievement, and consultants might tell you you're doing something wrong." She also noted that consultants are often not brought in unless there is existing pain, to the point where they have to admit they need help.

Dan Hamon works with tech organizations as a "fractional COO," a consultant who acts as a part-time chief operating officer of an organization. He explained during an interview how he has observed the technical leader's thought process: "I know something is wrong. I know I need help. I'll go to another STEM PhD for help because they're the only ones who can understand my business and my problems" (D. Hamon, personal communication, July 21, 2020). He also said that technical leaders are usually pragmatic, and if introduced by a trusted colleague to a consultant with technical and business expertise, the leader often moves forward to engage the right outside help for their needs. However, as explained in Chapter 1, this is rare. This chapter therefore presents a model to initiate consulting to technical leaders and use throughout the consulting process. It begins with how to attract their attention and gain credibility.

As shown in Figure 3.1, traditional ways of describing the organizational consulting process employ five major stages: (a) approach the client and agree on a contract, (b) collect data and make a diagnosis, (c) deliver feedback and make decisions to act, (d) implement the intervention, and (e) evaluate results and determine next steps or closure. A more simplified model is presented to highlight areas in which differences tend to arise when consulting to technical leaders. This model highlights four stages where differences occur: (a) attracting their attention to gain entry into the organization, (b) delivering the feedback from the diagnosis, (c) changing the way they think and do things during the implementation, and (d) evaluating the impact of the implementation (Block, 2011).

Figure 3.2 shows how two drivers tend to challenge the consultant at the various phases in specific ways. The two drivers are (a) resistance and

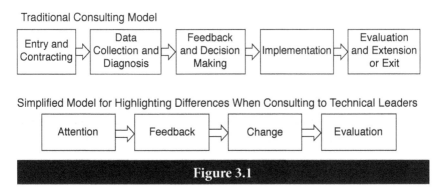

Figure 3.1

The general phases of organizational consulting.

(b) disconnect or lack of understanding. Resistance is a well-established element of organizational consulting that occurs when a client expresses reservations about the consultant's method or feedback in an indirect way, such as giving either too much detail or one-word answers, becoming silent or agreeing with everything, or repeatedly changing the subject (Block, 2011). All aspects of resistance apply to technical leaders, as they are humans just like the rest of us. However, for technical leaders, resistance manifests in particular ways that are worth noting. These are highlighted

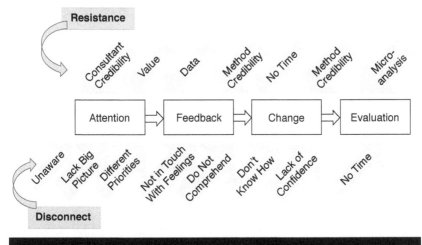

Figure 3.2

Challenges that arise during the consulting process with technical leaders.

in Figure 3.2; they are addressed in the following chapters in the context of the consulting phases and level of consulting.

In addition to overcoming resistance, another challenge arises for consultants that stems from the nature of technical leaders—their rational approach to life. A consultant in life sciences, Gaylene Xanthopoulos has developed thousands of leaders in the life sciences, from the boardroom to the bench. She has observed that they tend to make decisions on the bases of logic and fairness. She said this was a great quality, but it could also create challenges: For example, when someone has a different perspective than the leader's, the leader may respond with, "You must not understand, because otherwise you would agree with me" (G. Xanthopoulos, personal communication, April 20, 2020). She explained that this reaction could result in their getting stuck in one way of thinking and could, at times, lead to conflict.

The disconnect tends to emerge when organizational consultants emphasize (or overemphasize) abstract leadership concepts and intangible results or psychological issues, such as vulnerabilities and feelings (Berman, 2019; Leonard, 2017). It is hard to get someone's attention, understanding, or buy-in about leadership style, coaching techniques, and emotional issues if the person does not acknowledge the presence of these issues or see the immediate value of time and money spent on an intervention (Jack et al., 2013).

The attract–support–explain model shown in Figure 3.3 pinpoints three actions an organizational consultant can take to succeed in their consulting engagements with technical leaders. The first action is to attract

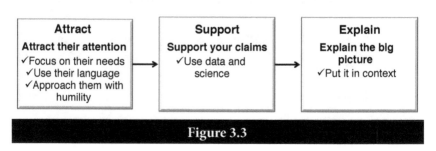

Figure 3.3

A model for organizational consultants to connect with technical leaders.

the attention of the technical leader; it is necessary during the entry phase of the engagement. Simply put, if the consultant does not attract the technical leader's attention and gain credibility, they will not get (or keep) the gig.

ATTRACT CLIENTS' ATTENTION

One challenge that may arise when consulting to technical leaders occurs when nontechnical issues are not a priority for them, and it can be hard to turn their attention toward people issues (Jack et al., 2013). This challenge first arises for organizational consultants during the entry phase. If a technical leader does not see the importance of your services, recognize how they apply, or even understand what you are talking about, you will not gain entry. As explained in Chapter 1, research shows that people in human resources (HR) and learning and development make limited progress with technical leaders when they offer generic leadership development and do not speak to the technical leaders' needs (BlessingWhite, 2013; DDI et al., 2018). My interview data suggested that organizational consultants and HR leaders succeed at working with technical leaders when they change their language and focus on the specific needs of technical leaders.

Focus on Clients' Perceived Needs

Technical leaders may not be aware of their needs or the possibilities for getting help outside the technical arena. A good place to start is by asking them what their challenges are. The research on technical leaders described in Chapter 1 and the interview excerpts with technical leaders in Chapter 2 and throughout the book shed some light on what technical leaders perceive as their primary challenges. Technical leaders tend to be most focused on delivering on their projects, and they are challenged with getting the technical talent and with training their teams on the technical skills they need to deliver. They are also challenged to balance delivering on their own responsibilities with managing people. Another point of stress for them is keeping up with and innovating in the technology that either is their company's business or makes their company's business possible.

Knowing the challenges that technical leaders face helps consultants target the questions to ask them and topics to offer them. For example, at the individual level, a consultant might ask the technical leader, "Are you challenged with balancing tech innovation and team management?" or "Are you losing too much time context switching?" At the group level, the question might be focused on factors that are putting the team at risk of not meeting their project goals. At the organizational level, the question might be, "Are you having difficulty attracting the tech talent you need?"

One consultant I interviewed had an example of steering a conversation with a leader in life sciences by focusing on the leader's needs for their team:

> The leader complained to me that his team wasn't efficient and there seemed to be a lot of duplication of effort. I brought the conversation around to trust building by leading with his concern: "You said you're frustrated with the duplication of efforts you're seeing on your team." I suggested if people trusted each other more, they could rely on each other for work, and they'd be more willing to communicate and share information. That allowed us to segue into how we could put together a team-building event. He was bought in with the value it would bring even though we were well on our way down the path of a psychological conversation. (Personal communication by an individual who did not wish to be cited by name, October 24, 2020)

Another approach is to learn the particular needs of an individual technical leader. Fawn Campbell, who works on the financial side of construction, shared her strategy of researching what an individual technical leader values and speaking to that for getting their attention:

> I research technical leaders to find out what they value first. What matters is what they're after. Take one of my largest developers, for example. His interest was getting more capital. That was the approach to open the door with him. A lot of times people pursue them on the social level, but I find the unique value that appeals to the technical

person. You need to show you do get it and you know what matters to them. That's critical for technical people. They may not care about what I do or what other players in the market do. They are very linear. I focus on that. (F. Campbell, personal communication, June 9, 2020)

As Ms. Campbell pointed out, a typical strategy for consultants is to develop personal relationships with organizational leaders to build business. While that may work in some industries, technical leaders seem to care more about value. Certainly, a personal relationship helps after it has been formed, but it is not necessarily a good way in. Technical leaders can be focused more on value than on friendship when they are making business decisions. They employ rational decision making and like to keep emotions out of it. They understand it is not personal or do not think about taking it personally (Chen & Simpson, 2015; Jack et al., 2013).

Use Clients' Language

Organizational consultants talk a lot about how their clients need to develop empathy, but we, as consultants, also need to employ empathy for our clients. We need to figuratively experience their situations from their viewpoints. That means shifting our way of thinking, doing, and speaking to match their way of thinking and speaking. It means thinking less about our jobs and more about theirs.

Kasey Harboe Guentert, a seasoned industrial and organizational (I/O) psychology consultant and internal HR leader, shared her wisdom from her work conducting job analyses:

A consultant should come to the job analysis process being really knowledgeable about the client product before launching the discussion about required skills. There are a couple of reasons; the job requirements change based on the nuances of each project and role, and also, it's important to build credibility with the subject matter experts. I've observed junior I/O psychologists and consultants arrive to focus group meetings with a 1980s-style job analysis questionnaire, asking engineers to describe the importance and frequency of

> generic tasks which are unrelated to the product and entirely lose credibility. The starting point should always be to listen, observe, and absorb, before trying to [put it in a] bucket and define [it]. (K. Harboe Guentert, personal communication, October 19, 2020)

The first step in using clients' language is to learn the terminology that they use. This terminology can be industry-specific language—for example, in the field of finance or science or computers, terminology describes methods, theories, products, tools, objects, regulations, and so on. It can also be organization specific. Many organizations have their own sets of acronyms and code names for projects, products, departments, and so on. In addition to the language of the industry and organization, there is language that deals with the way people work, such as the Agile software-development and Lean management philosophies that organizations employ to structure their work environments to be more productive and customer focused.

Learning clients' language facilitates understanding when listening to their challenges, but, more important, it builds credibility when speaking with them. Bill Berman, an accomplished organizational consultant who has worked with technical leaders for decades, emphasized the point during his interview with me:

> For the most part, you have to be good technically or they won't respect you. You have to prove to technical people that you know what they're doing. The fact that I can speak their language gives me the credibility to say that senior executives don't care about how technology works. (B. Berman, personal communication, May 7, 2020)

Technical leaders typically will not give consultants a lot of their already overscheduled time, so it is critical to use their language to get their attention up-front. Some have a terrible aversion to consultants. Harboe Guentert explained how it was easier for her to build relationships with technical leaders as an in-house service provider:

> As an external consultant, it was challenging to sell our assessments and competency design processes to tech start-ups. As an internal advisor, I have spent a lot more time with every stakeholder. I participate

in daily meetings, lunches, offsites, and there are random change projects I can jump in on and support. They see my face frequently,
so it builds trust, and they understand that I care about their program and their ability to be successful. My advice then becomes
a lot more credible. (K. Harboe Guentert, personal communication,
October 19, 2020)

How does a consultant learn the technical leader's language? There
are many ways to do this, such as reading books, industry magazines,
blogs, and company websites. A more active approach may include attending industry-specific conferences or group meetings or sitting in on their
meetings at work and listening to them talk to each other and taking notes
and looking up the words later. It takes extra time to research, read, and
take notes, but it is invaluable in building credibility with them. Additional tips might include listening for unfamiliar terms or acronyms and
researching them, distinguishing between meaningful process-based
language and less important technical jargon, and partnering with one
stakeholder who is willing to serve as an effective translator.

The following chapters in this book provide definitions of several terms
used in the STEM (science, technology, engineering, and mathematics)
fields, including Agile team methodology and the FDA drug approval
stages, and pointers to resources to learn more. Table 3.1 presents a summary of challenges that technical leaders reported experiencing at work
from the interview study reported in Chapter 2, in the language that technical leaders used in the interviews. The table also includes suggestions
for consultants to address the needs the leaders may have as a result of
these challenges.

Approach Technical Leaders With Humility

Recall that technical leaders are typically very smart people who know
a lot about their areas of expertise. Cassi Knight observed, "Technical
leaders pride themselves on being correct. That doesn't necessarily mean
they are, but it's seldom that they aren't. They are masters at what they do"
(C. Knight, personal communication, July 6, 2020). She said she does not

Table 3.1

Summary of Challenges and Resources for Technical Leaders

Challenge	Language	Needs	Consulting resources
People management			
Communicating upwards to make sure expectations are being met	My CEO, ensuring the issues that aren't identified as program risks are communicated to the program level, focusing on high-level initiatives	Communication skills, presentation skills, influencing skills, relationships, political savvy	Fournier, 2017; https://www.aldacenter.org/; Johns, 2019
Communicating to teams to make sure work is getting done and people understand what they need to do	Keeping people informed, expecting too much too quickly, having patience, struggling with poor performers, knowing what pitfalls may arise	Communication skills, listening skills, effective delegation skills, accountability process	Brahm and Kunze, 2012; Ferdman et al., 2021; Fournier, 2017; Jack et al., 2013
Motivating teams, managing conflict between team members and across functions, managing global teams	Ability to communicate the vision so people will understand, ability to dissect and break down the vision so people can understand, guiding people to follow the steps to accomplish the mission, making sure people leave a trail of their work and hand it off properly	Listening skills, empathy, emotional intelligence, coaching skills, help with team building, management of difficult conversations	Adkins, 2010; Bang and Midelfart, 2017; Covey, 2006; DeVilbiss and Gilbert, 2005; Mathieu et al., 2017; Socconini, and Reato, 2018
Performance management, dealing with poor performers	Underperforming people, poor performers, mentoring early career employees, knowing when to give a team member the chance to grow and when to let them go or exit	Talent management systems, skills for delivering feedback, accountability process, managing difficult conversations	Bang and Midelfart, 2017; Gøtzsche-Astrup, 2018; Hess, 2018; Rook et al., 2019; Scott, 2019

Table 3.1

Summary of Challenges and Resources
for Technical Leaders (*Continued*)

Challenge	Language	Needs	Consulting resources
Talent			
Recruiting, interviewing, getting the right talent on the team	Always be recruiting, having the right talent and having the right talent engaged, the average tenure of the developer is pretty short, always a fear of where next tech talent will come from, keeping talent, headcount shortage	Hiring, assessment, succession planning	Cappelli, 2019; Chen and Simpson, 2015; Ferdman et al., 2021; Ihsan and Furnham, 2018; Mundy, 2017; Nauta, 2010; Rounds et al., 2021
Making sure team members have the tech skills they need to complete projects, coaching, training	Training on my team, skill gaps, will an issue come up on my team that they're not trained for?	Training, mentoring	Johns, 2019; Leonard, 2017; Salicru, 2020; Sansone and Schreiber-Abshire, 2011; Vieth and Smith, 2008
Project delivery			
Checking details of work to make sure it is being done correctly	Exceed at all project obligations, keep dance card full with project work	Time management, accountability, prioritization	Appelo, 2016; Berman, 2019; Kendra and Taplin, 2004; Van den Berg and Pietersma, 2014

Note. Information is from participant responses in the interview study of technical leaders, organizational consultants, and human resources leaders conducted for this book.

get into a competition with them to prove them wrong. Rather, she said, "That would be a losing battle. Instead, I plant seeds. More often than not, I hear the idea reverberated to me a few months later. Their communication style is just different."

Another way to approach technical leaders is with humility, a willingness to learn, and a "help-first" attitude. Dan Hamon said that he volunteers or offers to take on something for them, like running a meeting, a side project, contributing to the technical workload, or assisting in recruitment, to name a few examples: "My strategy is to contribute, add value, learn, and actively form a hands-on working relationship that benefits that tech person" (D. Hamon, personal communication, July 21, 2020). He said they appreciate it, and little by little they warm up to him.

A more general consulting technique is to ask open-ended questions that take technical leaders out of their technical world and force them to talk about their feelings, their concerns, or the people side of things (Balser, 2019; Block, 2011; de Haan, 2019; Williams & Lowman, 2018). This approach is usually good if you already have the credibility to be sitting across the table from them—for example, if their manager or trusted colleague suggested they talk to you or you work for a highly reputable firm—or if they are at a retreat with nowhere to hide. It is also a way to be humble, making them the expert on the situation and demonstrating that you are simply there to listen and help them solve their problems.

Eric Roth has more than 25 years of leadership consulting experience at high-profile firms and has worked with many technical leaders. He said, "I built my credibility by asking them about their challenges, especially their challenges collaborating with other internal functions. These are typically more difficult than collaborating with the organization's customers and clients. Here I'm helping them learn politics" (E. Roth, personal communication, September 15, 2020). This approach lets the technical leader be the expert on their challenges and piques their attention by raising awareness of where they need help. It simultaneously establishes the consultant's expertise in leadership. The conversation becomes one of two experts in different fields talking to each other.

SUPPORT CLAIMS

Imagine a situation in which the consultant has piqued a technical leader's interest with a statement that addresses their needs. How does the leader know the consultant can offer them something useful?

Technical leaders are often skeptical and seldom take claims at face value. Any claims a consultant makes will need to be supported by data and evidence or logical, scientific explanations. For instance, when trying to get a technical leader's attention about needing to take notice of their stress levels, a consultant could use evidence about how many executives experience workplace stress—in a study of over 800 executives, 64% of them reported that their main source of stress was work related (Ganesh et al., 2018). Research on workplace stress repeatedly shows that employees' stress and burnout have negative effects on both employee health and organizational performance (Crawford et al., 2010). A recent meta-analysis of the burnout research showed that several workplace factors, such as ambiguous work expectations and work overload, could lead to burnout (Edmondson et al., 2019). The study also found that supervisory support and perceived organizational support were negatively associated with burnout. What that means is if you support your employees and give them clear expectations, you have a good chance of them not burning out.

Using science and facts may go against the grain for some organizational consultants. Some consultants may approach their clients immediately by empathizing and discussing feelings. That can be off-putting to tech people who are not so emotionally inclined. A client who values rational thinking above all else will likely either discount an emotionally driven person or put up a defensive wall to protect themself from being trapped in an uncomfortable conversation. Alternatively, they may miss the point entirely. Therefore, it is important for consultants to be able to take themselves out of the equation to connect with technical leaders on a different level. Ms. Knight described technical leaders as tending to be "introspective and not acting with emotion. They operate on data and you'd better be prepared with resources to back that data up" (C. Knight, personal communication, July 6, 2020). For her to interact with technical leaders, she continued, "It requires a little bit of preparation on my end. I need to speak their language, which means being direct and factual. No nonsense." In other words, she takes her emotions out of it and focuses on the facts to appeal to them.

Use Data

Higher level technical leaders may appreciate business metrics, such as budget, resources, employee turnover, and customer satisfaction. Consultants measure numerous outcomes, including tangible and intangible outcomes (Crabb, 2011; Salicru, 2020). In the stress and burnout example, a consultant could explain to a technical leader that burnout costs companies a lot of money because it leads to low engagement and employee turnover. The consultant could say to a leader, "If you burn out just one engineer on your team who earns $150,000 a year, and it typically costs one-and-a-half times their salary to replace them, it could cost the organization a quarter of a million dollars. Do you know the stress levels in your organization? We can assess that for you." This conversation is much different from one centered on how people feel. It is letting the numbers and data make the case. A common expression among technical leaders is: "The numbers speak for themselves." This is the appeal to them.

Mid- and low-level managers might prefer information that is related to how much stress will affect the team performance, not in dollars but in downtime or missed targets. For example, if an Agile team loses a developer during a "sprint" work cycle, the team may be in jeopardy of not making their sprint target. The dilemma becomes whether to redistribute the work to the other team members to meet the goal, at the risk of having them leave too, or to rescope the work, with the risk of disappointing the customer.

Consultants also benefit from knowing industry-specific metrics. Engineering metrics, for example, could include the changing size of the project or speed at which it is completed, what they might call "scope creep" or "sprint velocity." Life sciences metrics might include the lifetime of a product or how quickly they are spending their funding, what they might call "cycle time" or "burn rate." Service metrics for information technology (IT) and finance may include the quantity of requests for service—what they might call the "number of tickets"—as well as internal customer satisfaction. Building on these metrics, a consultant might say, "We could reduce the number of tickets (or problem reports) if IT had a better understanding of how the nurses were using the workstations. How can we increase their customer empathy (or awareness of customer needs)?"

Use Science

Science is often used to explain emotions to technical people. It is an effective way to explain how emotions play a role in decision making (Hambley, 2020). Stress, too, can be explained in a scientific way. For example, a training for a technical team could include a scientific explanation of the effects of stress on the body: Acute stress is the reaction a person has to a perceived threat, like being criticized in a meeting, having an argument with a loved one, or being told to do a dreadful task. When the threat is perceived, the amygdala is activated to automatically trigger the autonomic nervous system to enter the fight-or-flight mode. That causes muscles to tense, heart rate to increase, breathing to slow, and cognitive focus to narrow (Goleman, 1994). It also causes the adrenal glands to produce cortisol to increase the level of energy available. The body is meant to handle temporary stressors, but not chronic stress. When the body is in constant defense mode, it stays tense, the cardiovascular system continues to work extra hard, cortisol remains high, and the whole body is strained (Walker, 2019). Research shows that long periods of stress can lead to burnout, and burnout can cause permanent, irreparable damage to the body, such as heart disease, Type 2 diabetes, and chronic pain (American Psychological Association, 2018; Mayo Clinic Staff, 2021). Technical leaders will likely appreciate a detailed explanation of the physiology of emotions before exploring the psychological aspects.

Explain the Big Picture

As described in Chapter 1, technical leaders typically are under intense pressure to deliver on complex, rapidly changing project goals. They have to be focused to succeed, and they may not necessarily contemplate the bigger picture of which their work is but one part. If a consultant comes in waving standard business metrics to get a technical leader's attention, it may not work. David Oates is a crisis public relations consultant who often works with technical leaders when they run into trouble, for example when the FDA does not approve their latest test or their start-up does not get the next round of funding it needs. When I interviewed him, he explained:

> They don't pay attention to the typical metrics like employee turn-over and the ability to innovate. In tech and biotech, the goal is to get the product to market and get a decent EBIDA [earnings before interest, depreciation, and amortization], and they don't look at turn-over. Investors don't look at that either. It's cheaper to innovate on your own but you need to invest in long-term gain. Google does that well; they invest in innovation. (D. Oates, personal communication, April 6, 2020)

Part of the "sell" may be drawing the technical leader's attention to the bigger goals and concerns of the organization. It may require, for example, making the link between a technical issue and an organizational goal explicit rather than assuming they see the relevance, especially if others in the organization are tasked with running the business side of things. For example, the clinical development team in a pharmaceutical company may not be collaborating with manufacturing. What is the larger effect of this dysfunctional relationship? The product might be delayed to market. The effects may be even broader than the profitability of the company. Every day that the product is not available to patients, lives may be lost. If a team is dysfunctional, taking a day off for an intervention may stop these delays from happening and thereby help to save lives.

SUMMARY

Although organizational consulting is fundamentally the same across organizational and industry contexts, consultants may benefit from adapting the traditional consulting process to address certain challenges that can arise when consulting to technical leaders. Organizational consulting starts with gaining access to the organization and getting buy-in from the leader(s) involved. In the context of technical leaders, certain approaches are more effective than others. Technical leaders are well versed in logic and data, and consultants will likely find scientific, logic-based, and data-driven tools and explanations to be more appealing to their clients. The attract–support–explain model, shown in Figure 3.3, incorporates modifications to traditional approaches that work with leaders in STEM, including focusing on their needs, using their language, and appreciating their way of thinking. I advise consultants to think of these approaches as tools to select from, using the best one for each particular scenario. I suggest they not use tools that do not resonate with them. Rather, as Bellman (1990) suggested, it is better for a consultant to be themselves, to use their skills and tweak the tools to suit their needs.

4

Consulting at the Individual Level: Creating Effective Engagement With Technical Leaders

This chapter focuses on what happens after the consultant has entered the organization, agreed to work with an individual technical leader, and signed a contract to provide assessment, coaching, or other intervention. It describes the feedback and change phases of the consulting model with technical leaders at the individual level. Individual-level consulting often consists of assessment and development, and it is typically conducted in a coaching engagement, which includes both (Lowman, 2016). I begin with a case example of an executive-level technical leader and use that as a basis for highlighting common issues that come up in coaching engagements, as shown in Figure 3.2, and common topics of coaching. Subsequently, I review other individual development methods that have been shown to be effective for technical leaders.

https://doi.org/10.1037/0000270-005
Consulting to Technical Leaders, Teams, and Organizations: Building Leadership in STEM Environments, by J. B. Connell

COACHING TECHNICAL LEADERS

The following case example illustrates several components of a proto-typical individual-level consulting engagement with a technical client. As described in the Introduction, the case is a composite of several typical clients, and any potentially identifiable information has been disguised to protect client confidentiality.

Case Example: A Neurosurgeon in Trouble

Dr. S was one of the top neurosurgeons in the country, the smartest doctor in his hospital, viewed as being a commanding leader. In fact, his ability to take charge and move quickly was exactly what led him to success in the operating room and had brought him to be the head of his division. In the operating room, he moved swiftly and tended to bark orders to the team. He believed he had to do that or the patient might die. He felt that he needed to make quick decisions and get the right tools with which to operate without taking time to see what others thought or to exchange pleasantries. Focus and accuracy are essential in this type of work. Dr. S was incredibly smart, but he had little patience for others to keep up with his rapid understanding and decision making. He also publicly called out others' mistakes, even though it often hurt people's feelings, because he felt that people needed to learn how to do things right. The residents and staff feared him, got out of his way when he walked down the hall, and ran to each other for consolation after one of his reprimands.

The hospital's reputation and revenue depended in a large part on Dr. S since his reputation brought in a steady flow of referrals. Because of that, he was perceived as being untouchable, so those who found his manner objectionable complained only to each other, not to him directly. The officer-level executives (i.e., C-Suite leaders) were afraid of an employ-ment or malpractice lawsuit because of the way he treated people, but they did not ask him to change because they felt the pressure to bring in revenue, particularly when revenues were otherwise down. Those results really mat-tered for donors and rankings, and the C-Suite leaders were hesitant to disrupt the revenue stream. The leaders wanted him to change, but they had not required it. They were under a lot of pressure, however, because the health care industry had been experiencing a great reform. Changes in regulatory control, research, patient care, operational costs, ethics, and training were several major influences that had been affecting health care leadership for some time, and at the hospital they were not acting according to current standards (Black, 2006; Dagi, 2017). Whereas neurosurgeons in Dr. S's early days were used to being the "king" of the OR and chief of staff, health care reform has changed what health care organizations expect of them (Dye & Garman, 2015). They are now expected to be collaborative, flexible leaders who are team members rather than sovereigns. Dr. S was not adapting to these changes, and the colleagues with whom he was supposed to be collaborating found it impossible to do so.

The situation came to a head when the chief development officer announced to the executive team that he could not bring Dr. S into any more fundraising meetings. He said that efforts had failed, and Dr. S was unaware that his condescending and insulting behavior had largely been the cause. The C-Suite was starting to realize that Dr. S was negatively affecting the hospital.

The chief people officer (CPO) was charged with his reform. The CPO explained to the consultant that Dr. S was surprised when he had been told that if he did not change his behavior, he would be terminated from the hospital. He had brushed it off by saying, "But I'm the most famous neurosurgeon in the country!" He seemed to think he was entitled to behave in the way that he did because he was so valuable. The CPO sought a coach to help Dr. S understand the impact of his behavior and make the necessary changes to his leadership approach to succeed in the new health care environment. As would soon be evident to the coach, the hospital also needed help managing the organizational transition during the health care reform, but they had not acknowledged it yet.

This kind of entitlement and lack of awareness may sound extreme, but I have found that it is not uncommon in technical industries in which technical experts really are highly prized. As an organizational consultant and engineer by training, I have witnessed it frequently. One place where this topic arises frequently is in my interviews with technical leaders on my *Reinventing Nerds* podcast. One technical leader, Geoffrey Mattson, CEO of MistNet, described his experiences with techno-entitlement in Silicon Valley, saying that nerds grow up as "spoiled children" and have a "nerd privilege" (Connell, 2018). He and several other technical leaders have admitted that they grappled with those feelings themselves and described how they either worked through or overcame them to help their teams be more successful.

The Coach's Challenges

In this case, Dr. S had received feedback, but he did not even see why it was relevant, much less understand the difficulties his behavior was creating. If a consultant were to assess him, either through a 360-degree-feedback tool to solicit feedback from his supervisor, peers, and subordinates or with an external assessment instrument to better understand his leadership skills, he might attack the validity of the instrument or want to know who provided the ratings and pick them apart one by one. If he were to be convinced that the threat of being fired was real, he would likely not know what he needed to do differently. He would need specific instructions regarding exactly what to say and do differently, what to look for in other people's reactions, and how to ask them for what they want from him. It would also take a fundamental shift in his leadership style to move from commanding and controlling to being democratic when outside of the operating room. Making these changes could put him in a very uncomfortable position—not being completely confident and in control of his situation.

Although, as discussed in Chapter 3, consulting to technical leaders is not fundamentally different from consulting to other types of leaders, certain issues tend to arise frequently in working with such leaders, and certain consulting approaches are likely to be more successful with them. As shown in Figure 3.2, organizational consultants working with technical leaders may run into specific challenges in two areas: resistance and disconnect. Because technical leaders tend to have a different approach or mindset from organizational consultants, they may oppose consultants' methods or not understand them. In a coaching engagement, resistance and disconnect will surface during the feedback and change phases. When coaching technical leaders, it can be helpful to remember this simple phrase: resolve the resistance and dissolve the disconnect. In other words, working through opposition and clarifying misunderstandings are part of each stage of the consulting engagement. Some techniques for this purpose are described in the sections that follow.

Resolving Resistance When Giving Feedback to Technical Leaders

Technical people may be accustomed to getting feedback on the content of their ideas and on the correctness of their work but not on their behaviors. It is the rare exception when a technical person has received valuable feedback from their manager. Those who have received such guidance often report feeling very fortunate to work for such a good manager (Hurd, 2009). Even in technical teams that follow the Agile philosophy (see Chapter 5), in which people are supposed to give each other feedback during their "retrospective" meetings, it may not be done effectively.

Soliciting and receiving feedback can be anxiety provoking for people who are not used to it, but technical people tend to respond well to methods that required them to "gather data" to use in their decision making, such as identifying situations that trigger frustration and understanding the organizational context to help them prepare in advance (e.g., Hurd, 2009; Johns, 2019; Rook et al., 2019). Some consultants might call this "building self-awareness" or "getting in touch with emotions," but the language of gathering data will likely be less intimidating for people who are not used to thinking in those terms.

A word of caution: Feedback data can be a problem for technical people. As described in Chapter 1, technical people have typically been rewarded for having the right answers throughout their careers, and they are used to thinking categorically. When someone gives them feedback, they may jump to the conclusion that someone is telling them they are wrong and feel compelled to argue for why they are right. Consultants need to be prepared to help technical leaders work through their defensiveness and to allow time for that process to unfold.

When Data Serve as Resistance

Consultants to technical leaders can end up going down a rabbit hole, feeling forced to prove that the feedback they provided is accurate. Technical leaders generally love data and want evidence to support claims. When resistant technical leaders like Dr. S are given feedback that they are behaving too abrasively, they might request data on the percentage of interactions they had over the last year in which others characterized them as being "abrasive." Alternatively, they might want evidence to support specific instances. When a specific example is provided, such as when Dr. S raised his voice at the head nurse who he said was in the way, a technical leader might demand more examples. Dr. S might also say that other nurses with whom he worked were not bothered by him, and he would likely cast aspersions on the nurse in the example provided.

Seasoned consultants will have seen all sorts of resistance to feedback and may not be surprised by this reaction. However, the persistence of technical leaders' resistance can be more than average, and their way of interpreting feedback as either correct or incorrect can be challenging to navigate. Part of their reaction may stem from having to be correct, either about the actions or about refuting the statements at hand. Another part might reflect concern with the details and a desire to dig as deep as possible. Both reactions miss the point. In my experience, the following method has been useful in addressing such resistance: I start by agreeing with clients that the data could be incorrect. Then I either ask them what else may be going on or ask them to consider, hypothetically, if there were some semblance of truth embedded in this feedback, what do they think it would be referring to? In any case, disarming them of the argument about the correctness of the data can be a good way to keep the client focused on the content of the feedback.

When the Credibility of the Method Serves as Resistance

An expression of resistance that can arise with technical people, due to their generally investigative, precise, analytical nature, is to attack the credibility of the assessment method (Chen & Simpson, 2015). If it is a 360-degree feedback tool, for example, they may raise questions about the quality of the instrument or the items or the number of participants. Some consultants send the technical specifications of the assessment instrument to the client ahead of the meeting to give credence to the method. Others identify and confront the resistance and redirect the leader to the content of the feedback. Either way, it is a good idea to be armed with the technical specs of the instrument in case clients insist on seeing them or to have a few statistics about the instrument put to memory. Being able to report that the personality test has a Cronbach's alpha of .82 internal consistency reliability or that a cognitive ability measure has a .51 predictive validity with job performance can be effective in responding to concerns without the primary purposes for the assessments getting waylaid.

On the other hand, a consultant may be using a different kind of instrument, such as a 360-degree feedback instrument or a work style inventory for which the statistics are not the point. In this case, focusing on the qualitative data and context might be a better approach. For example, in a 360-degree feedback, focusing on the comments made by the raters or examples of how a competency is used on the job makes the feedback directly relevant to success at work. It may help to do a focused exploration with the client on how they think the comment or comments show up rather than to assume the client makes the link. The simple question of "how does this show up at work" is a powerful one for getting the conversation started and eventually for their being able to understand why the feedback is relevant.

Resistance also occurs when technical people do not see the value of the work consultants do or how complex it is. Will Marshall, an attorney focusing on technology transactions, explained it well during an interview I conducted for this book:

> Tech people often don't feel appreciated for how complex their stuff is, but they have a blind spot of the complexity of other people's stuff. For example, with my legal work, they can be easily dismissive of it. It's ironic because they're sensitive to [feeling underappreciated] themselves. (W. Marshall, personal communication, April 8, 2020)

Sometimes the work that organizational consultants do can seem obvious or silly and may be easily dismissed. It may be worth taking a little time to give some context or research findings about feedback in organizations to shift their mindset. A good source for that purpose is Gregory and Levy's (2015) book, *Using Feedback in Organizational Consulting.*

Dissolving the Disconnect When Giving Feedback to Technical Leaders

Organizational consultants may sometimes be surprised at how little self-awareness technical leaders have and how little understanding they have of their interpersonal behavior and its effects on others (Chen & Simpson, 2015; Jack et al., 2013; Rasoal et al., 2012). In the interview study described in Chapter 2, for example, two of the 25 technical leaders I interviewed for this book said, "I don't know" when asked, "What leadership skills would you like to develop?" Consultants may want to probe to uncover when a technical leader is resisting as opposed to simply not understanding feedback.

The Disconnect of Not Being in Touch With Feelings

Because technical leaders may not be in touch with their feelings, sometimes feedback may fall flat (Chen & Simpson, 2015; Sánchez-Ruiz et al., 2010). Some technical leaders may have never really thought about the feelings that underlie their actions or the reasons that they may be in a bad mood. Some may not have the emotional vocabulary to articulate what they or others are feeling. For example, when the feedback is that they are too argumentative, overly critical, or heated with others, such a person may not understand what that means or how it feels or why it matters.

Kathy, a director in a medical devices company, was referred to me by the company's human resources (HR) director for coaching. She was having conflicts at work. Kathy had a habit of blaming other people on her project teams for poor performance during our initial coaching conversations. When I probed into what the other team members were doing poorly, she said they did not do what she said. She gave an example of telling one person to file something by a certain date and later finding out he had not done so. In further discussions of the example during the third coaching session, she mentioned in passing that she "may have raised her voice" with this person when she discovered he had not performed as directed. She added that she was frustrated and sick of working with people who were not competent. Then she broke down in tears. Up until that point in the coaching, she had not consciously experienced or expressed her anger and frustration. She just behaved as if it were reasonable to yell at someone who had not done what they were told.

Asking the right questions is an important part of getting technical leaders to gradually address the disconnect with discussing their feelings. David Schmaltz, organizational consultant and author of *The Blind Men and the Elephant*, explained when I interviewed him, "Technical leaders have a strong belief in technology. They believe if you're really smart you can think your way through anything. I ask questions that do not ask them to think. I seek their perspective rather than their knowledge" (D. Schmaltz, personal communication, December 16, 2019). Getting their perspective can be a way to open the door to a follow up question about how they feel about something. Schmaltz called these "the F questions," where "F" stands for feelings. He described F questions as "questions that require access to feelings to answer to get them away from knowledge. For example, how does this difficulty feel to you? What annoys you? What keeps you awake at 3 a.m.?"

Bringing tools to help clients understand what can cause emotions and how they are felt—especially more subtle ones—and what words to use to describe them can be very helpful. For example, graphics depicting the Anger Iceberg and bodily maps of emotions are easy to print out or pop up on a tablet during a feedback meeting (Benson, 2016; Nummenmaa et al., 2014). The Anger Iceberg is a tool that originated in the field of couples therapy but has been found to be useful to help people in nontherapeutic settings, such as at school and work, identify what is driving anger (e.g., being exhausted, stressed, grumpy, feeling attacked, hurt, worried). Common sources of anger, such as hurt and shame, are superimposed onto the iceberg, and most of them are below the surface of the water, representing they are not typically immediately identifiable. Nummenmaa and colleagues (2014) created simple graphic outlines of humans to show how and where in the body people feel emotions. Different colors represent the intensity of where an emotion is typically felt. For example, anger is typically felt as a strong activation of the muscles in the head, chest, shoulders, and arms, whereas fear is typically felt as a strong activation in the chest and some in the head, hands, and gut. Even if the leader disagrees with the maps, it is a good way to have a conversation about emotions and how the individual experiences them.

The Disconnect of Not Comprehending the Feedback

An organizational consultant told a story about a VP of clinical development at a pharmaceutical company who asked them about a statistically significant difference between the self and manager rating on a 360-degree feedback competency. The VP wanted to measure improvement by reducing the discrepancy between the two ratings by 10%. The consultant told him a 360 instrument did not have enough reliability to do that level of analysis and tried to focus him on the point of the 360 rather than the details of the data. Meanwhile, the consultant asked the HR director what kinds of performance metrics they were already using in the organization that they might be able to use to help demonstrate improvement. She said, practically speaking, that moving his team from dysfunction to function would be a measure of success. The disconnect was not that a brilliant scientist could not understand 360-degree feedback. It occurred because he was looking at the instrument through a different lens—the scientific lens of precision to which he was accustomed—and not through an interpersonal lens to understand why the manager viewed the behavior differently.

A different kind of miscomprehension occurs when clients do not understand the gravity of their problematic behavior. For example, in the case discussed at the beginning of this chapter, Dr. S seemed not to understand the seriousness of his situation, even after he received the feedback. It did not occur to him that he could actually be fired. From his perspective, he had been behaving the same way for many years and had never been counseled or reprimanded about it, so it seemed to him unlikely that they would do something now. This kind of disconnect can occur in other STEM industries as well. One engineer described it as "techno-entitlement," a situation in which people feel they are so valuable because of their technical skills that they do not have to treat people well. If they do not take the threat of being fired seriously, they will generally not take the coaching seriously either. As a coach, it might therefore be wise to get the organization to make the potential consequences of termination clear to the person to help them understand that change is necessary.

Resolving Resistance When Working With Technical Leaders on Change

Making changes can be hard for everyone, but the kinds of changes organizational consultants propose can be particularly challenging for technical leaders to embrace. Being oriented to analytical thinking and logic, technical leaders may not be accustomed to incorporating feelings into their decisions, and they may be missing critical information as a result. It can be an uphill battle to get them to consider stepping outside of a purely logical approach, but it is very important to respect the values of the scientist and let them keep their identities. The idea is to open up technical leaders' thinking and awareness to see what other points of data to consider and other tools they can use in a way that fits with their personality and style (Sánchez-Ruiz et al., 2010; Sato, 2016).

As with anyone facing change, technical leaders may put up barriers to modifying their way of thinking or behaving (Crosby, 2021; Kahneman, 2013; Leonard, 2017; Rathmell et al., 2019). Two of the most common reasons technical leaders use for not changing are that they are too busy and that they have more important things to focus on at the moment. These concerns are often true. As described in Chapter 1, technical leaders tend to feel a great deal of pressure to meet project goals. Consequently, leadership development is not seen as a pressing need, and it is often pushed off until later. Even so, some of the procrastination stems from resistance to change.

Lack of Time as Resistance

Here is an example of how lack of time can serve as an excuse for not dealing with problematic behavior by technical managers. Suppose a company has a board meeting at the end of the month, a product's FDA approval is coming up, and the company's fiscal quarter ends the following week.

Because lack of time is such a reasonable excuse for technical leaders not to take on new tasks linked to an intervention, an unsuspecting consultant can be strung along. The typical consulting approach would be to call them out on their pushback, and that may be the best approach to resolve their resistance. However, the consultant may also consider other approaches. The consultant's explanation of how interpersonal behavior changes will actually help them meet their goal can be effective because their task focus may have prevented them from seeing the potential changes as things to make their work lives better (Jack et al., 2013). For example, consultants can help their clients see how development is an investment, not a cost; how an hour spent now might save them 10 hours later; or how investing in a few minutes of personal conversation at the beginning of a meeting, even one held in the midst of urgent deadlines, can build rapport, decrease stress levels, and "grease the wheels" for a much more productive outcome.

However, the leader's anxiety around meeting their impending deadline might be so high that it may be impossible to break through to them. Sometimes, in such cases, it may be better to ask the client when they can work on the intervention. The consultant can then obtain a firm commitment beginning after the imminent deadlines. For example, the consultant may agree to delay the next coaching session for 3 weeks, but each party can put the meeting on their calendar for a specific time for which there is a commitment. Shorter, more targeted development, like brief coaching engagements of three to six sessions, may be effective for such circumstances, especially when working with technical leaders in small companies with fast-moving targets and low budgets (de Haan, 2019). Conducting coaching by phone or video can also save time and slip into a leader's schedule more easily.

However, downsides to shortening engagements and consultations have shown up in the coaching literature (de Haan, 2019). For example, short engagements may not provide enough of an intervention or may not be sufficiently frequent to sustain attention and practice and to facilitate lasting change. Short meetings may impair the coach's ability to develop a relationship with the client. Short, task-focused meetings do not model to the client the importance of building relationships for leaders who, more than likely, do not take time for that in their other meetings either. Technical leaders tend to be fast learners if they are motivated, though, so short, targeted engagements can be very successful.

Method Credibility as Resistance

Another common consulting challenge occurs when technical leaders do not agree with the suggested methodology for change. For example, a consultant may run into resistance when suggesting that a technical leader build rapport with the team members by showing an interest in their personal lives. Clients may respond that they are just not interested in people's personal lives and it would not be authentic for them to fake it. Dr. S would likely say that. Similarly, they might balk at the suggestion of sharing their feelings with someone or to work on building their emotional intelligence. Consultants can identify resistance when clients repeatedly shoot down the consultant's suggestions or criticize the provided change tools.

Many consulting books and articles describe effective ways to work through client resistance (e.g., Block, 2011). They typically involve confronting resistance and talking through clients' underlying concerns. I fully support this approach, and I offer another option that works with technical leaders who are not ready or willing to talk through their fears and concerns: I have found that asking technical leaders what has worked for them in the past or what they have tried that did not work, and why it did or did not work, is an effective way to steer the conversation from resistance to a more productive direction. Directing clients to talk about their past experiences can help them identify their concerns and help them generate solutions for their technical environments.

Dissolving the Disconnect When Working With Technical Leaders on Change

When clients do not appear to be resisting but seem genuinely confused or to have hit a dead end because they do not understand aspects of the change intervention, organizational consultants may find it appropriate to employ one of the following methods to dissolve the disconnect.

The Disconnect of Not Knowing How

Many coaches have been taught never to offer solutions to clients and only to ask questions. The philosophy is that the clients have the answers themselves and the consultant's job is to facilitate their finding those answers. Although this philosophy may apply to some consulting situations, it is not necessarily what technical people want or expect from a coaching engagement. Technical leaders are used to using tools, processes, and systems to achieve results. Reflecting questions back to them may cause frustration and blank stares. Two common examples that draw pause are asking a technical leader how they would go about coaching a direct report without telling them what to do and what other ways they could influence someone besides using data. At times, trying to draw ideas out of technical leaders can feel laborious to the consultant. It may seem as if the client is fighting the consultant, but that is not always the case. Being very literal and precise, technical leaders may not want to get the answer wrong, in which case they may not say anything.

One effective strategy to dissolve the disconnect and start the conversation is to bring a "toolkit" of sorts and see what resonates with them. Some consultants find it helpful to show clients a list of many options to choose among and/or provide the client books and other resources, especially resources created by other technical people. For example, Kaminsky's (2012) article in the *Journal of Leadership Studies*, "Impact of Nontechnical Leadership Practices on IT Project Success," contains a list of leadership practices (described later in this chapter) that are presented in the words of other technical leaders. Bradberry and Greaves's (2009) book, *Emotional Intelligence 2.0*, and its companion book, *Leadership 2.0* (Bradberry, 2012), have several lists of behaviors that people can use to increase emotional intelligence and improve adaptive leadership skills. Fournier's (2017) book, *The Manager's Path*, also presents many suggestions for people interactions, including a list of questions to build trust and rapport with a new team member. If a client does not find a resource that suits them, the consultant can take the opportunity to bring the conversation back to what they think would work for them or what has worked for them in the past.

The Disconnect of Not Being Confident

It is ironic to talk about technical experts lacking confidence. They generally do not lack confidence when working in their areas of expertise (e.g., Walker, 2019). However, when their value in the organization shifts from getting things done to managing people, they may be in unfamiliar territory. It is generally not their expertise—yet. Managing people calls for a different set of skills that have to be learned (Chen & Simpson, 2015; Rasoal et al., 2012; Rounds et al., 2021).

Delegating for technical leaders can be challenging because it means letting go of the details and having others handle the science and technology, their areas of expertise and comfort (Greiner, 1998). Technical leaders may find influencing others to do things to be challenging because, without specific training, they may feel that methods of influence are not based on a scientific or evidence-based course of action, even when they are. Delivering and receiving honest feedback can be challenging because they require social agility, comfort with ambiguity, and courage to initiate difficult conversations, which technical leaders may yet to have acquired. These new ways of doing things are viewed as nontechnical. When people who are used to feeling ultraconfident and "right" are thrown into situations with which they do not have experience, it can be very unsettling, and leading from a place of insecurity often produces unpleasant results.

In addition, unlike in the technical space, good leadership can appear to be hard to measure. It is not whether the code works, or the FDA approved the treatment, or the balance sheet adds up. Many technical leaders experience a moment of panic when they do not know what their performance metrics look like and they do not know if they are meeting expectations. Additionally, much of people management is subtle; it is not black and white. People's behaviors are not as predictable as technology, and people often do not behave in logical ways. The lack of consistency may be one of the reasons why clients chose their technical occupations—to avoid having to deal with murky people interactions.

Like most people, technical leaders will likely need encouragement and confidence building when trying to learn new skills, in this case, leading. However, because some technical leaders are smart, well educated, and possibly uncomfortable revealing that they do not know something or have not done it before, consultants need sensitivity and tact. Part of the coaching process may simply be helping clients to become comfortable with saying "I don't know" and then being willing to learn.

It is necessary for the coach to understand another important point about technical leaders. Typically being quick thinkers, technical leaders may not have a great deal of patience, both with themselves and with the results they seek when they are ready to change (Walker, 2019). As high achievers, they may be tempted to take on too much too quickly. Helping to slow them down and to lower their expectations without being perceived as insulting them can be tricky. One strategy that works well is to have a standard process for change with small, measurable steps of achievement along the way (Kendra & Taplin, 2004).

The "Scientific Method" Coaching Process for Technical Leaders

A specific coaching framework that is a potentially effective method and has reportedly worked with technical leaders is Hurd's (2009) six-step process that parallels the scientific method. The idea is that presenting leadership development to technical people as a parallel to a scientific process helps them feel more comfortable with the process. The six steps of the scientific method generally can be described as (a) start with a research problem or question, (b) conduct background research to see what is currently known, (c) formulate a hypothesis, (d) conduct an experiment to test the hypothesis, (e) analyze the results, and (f) draw conclusions and posit future inquiries. The six steps of Hurd's coaching process are summarized as (a) state the broad objective of the coaching engagement, (b) gather feedback and assessment data to help the leader be more aware of their current behavior and its impact, (c) develop goals and specific action steps for new behavior, (d) experiment with the new behaviors, (e) discuss the outcomes, and (f) conduct an evaluation and develop a plan for the future.

This process is essentially what organizational consultants already do; it is not new. What is unique is the way it is presented to scientifically trained leaders. For example, a consultant might explain the coaching process to a technical leader by saying,

> We'll take a scientific approach to the engagement. It is probably similar to what you do in your work. We'll start by conducting some background research to find out where you are at now in your leadership performance, then put together a couple of hypotheses on what kinds of changes might make the most positive impact for improved performance, and then test these hypotheses. The tests will be you trying out new behaviors and seeing how well they work. Just as with science, behavior change typically needs a few iterations to get it right.

This language illustrates the "use their language" section of the attract–support–explain model that was presented in Chapter 3.

COMMON LEADERSHIP DEVELOPMENT TOPICS FOR TECHNICAL LEADERS

In the first two chapters, I presented many of the challenges that technical leaders face, both from the literature and from interviews with technical leaders that I conducted for this book. In this section, I focus on areas that organizational consultants and other leadership development professionals have identified as development opportunities for technical leaders. In Table 4.1, I summarize the issues that organizational consultants and HR leaders reported as commonly arising during coaching engagements with technical leaders and the topics of coaching conversations that often emerged. Next, I review several leadership models and development frameworks that were created specifically for technical leaders.

Technical Leadership Models and Development Frameworks

Technical leadership development frameworks differ from generic leadership approaches in that they are typically created to address specific needs of technical leaders. They tend to include technical competencies, and some are even industry specific, such as health care or information technology (IT)

Table 4.1

Common Issues That Arise During Coaching Engagements With Technical Leaders

Issue	Conversations may center on
Ambiguity, unknown expectations	Changing roles, like CIO versus CTO; performance expectations of managers; defining roles, responsibilities, and decision-making processes; challenges of matrix management
Not letting go	Managing the need for control and perfectionism; identity as a scientist and as a doer; differences in performance metrics for managers and individual contributors
Business acumen	Budgets; setting a vision for the team; aligning with the organizational vision; focusing on business strategy and the big picture; risk management for the organization
Empathy and awareness	Emotional intelligence; emotional components of decision making; building rapport and relationships with team and with key players
Communication	Presentation skills; speaking to people outside their function; listening; increasing the quantity of communication to clarify expectations and build accountability
Collaboration	Building trust; incentivizing teamwork; coaching others on how to collaborate; big picture/organizational goals
Coaching and developing team members	How much more they can get done if they empower others to do it; asking versus telling; motivating people through development; difficult conversations; giving and receiving feedback
Time management and prioritizing	Identifying what is important; building a capable team to delegate; how to say no

Note. Information is from participant responses in the interview study of technical leaders, organizational consultants, and human resources leaders conducted for this book. CIO = chief information officer; CTO = chief technology officer.

leadership competencies. Another important factor is that because they are specifically tailored to technical leaders, participants can feel at home and authentically explore their leadership styles rather than being thrust into generic leader roles. In the sections following, I describe three representative technical leadership models.

The SERC Leadership Framework

The Systems Engineering Research Center (SERC) is a university-affiliated research center of the U.S. Department of Defense that draws on senior lead systems engineering researchers from 22 collaborator universities across the United States. A team of researchers examined literature and case examples of several large, complex technical organizations to develop a technical leadership development framework that helps leaders develop both the technical skills and the leadership skills needed to be successful as technical leaders. The framework was intended for the Department of Defense (or other government or nongovernment organizations) to use to develop their technical leaders (Felder et al., 2016).

Felder et al.'s (2016) leadership framework has three career stages: junior (management of self), mid-level (management of others), and senior (management of managers). It has 24 competencies, 12 "technical" and 12 "enabling" or leadership-focused competencies. The technical competencies focus on the thinking, planning, and product development aspects of work while the enabling competencies tend to embody standard leadership competencies that one would see in any number of leadership textbooks. The competencies are tailored to each career stage. There are six methods of leadership development—education, training, experience, job rotations, mentoring, and coaching—which should be used in varying degrees at each career stage. The idea is that a technical person would progress through the three different career stages and achieve proficiency in the competencies at one stage before moving to the next.

This framework for leadership development is fairly standard for large organizations with functioning learning and development departments. The unique value is the competency model that is a valid research-based model that includes both technical and leadership components. In fact, each competency has both a technical and a leadership rationale. For example, the "technical" competency of technical planning is important because "technical planning requires understanding the technical activities in order to plan them accurately" (Felder et al., 2016, p. 33). It is important to leadership because "technical plans provide direction to subordinate organizations and inform superior organizations" (p. 52). The "enabling" competency of developing people is important because "it counteracts the senior level leader's technical tendency to focus predominantly on the task and associated technical processes to a focus on the people and associated development processes" (p. 52). It is important to leadership because it is "a key component of the traditional leadership lexicon" (p. 52) of coaching, mentoring, succession planning, and supporting growth.

Google's 8 Key Management Behavior Model

Google took a completely different approach to develop their management training program than SERC did. Google stayed inwardly focused, insisting that they did things uniquely within their company. Originally, their philosophy of management was that the manager's role was to stay out of the way and empower employees to make decisions (Scott, 2019). Google's founders, Larry Page and Sergey Brin, even wondered for a while whether managers were necessary at all. In 2002, for example they eliminated all their engineering manager positions to create a completely flat, more collegial organization because they thought managers might be more destructive than beneficial (Garvin, 2013). What they found was the opposite: Managers were necessary, and they had to bring them back.

In 2008, Google researchers embarked on Project Oxygen, a project designed to determine the behaviors exhibited by effective managers at Google. They analyzed data from performance reviews, employee surveys, employee interviews, and so on, and found eight behaviors of the best Google managers. The behaviors can be summarized as coaching team members, caring about them, helping them with career development, not micromanaging, being results oriented, communicating, having clear vision and strategy, and having technical skills (Bryant, 2011; Garvin, 2013). These behaviors guided the creation of Google's management development programs (Google, 2020b).

Although the company had gone to great lengths to uncover the secrets of effective management at Google, what the researchers discovered were behaviors of good managers everywhere. Even though Google is a technical company, the findings applied to their managers in general, not just the technical managers—although being technically competent was a key attribute. Six of the key behaviors were about people, one was about business, and only one concerned technical skills. This is not to say that technical skills were not important, because they were. However, technical skills were just one of the eight key attributes of an effective manager at Google.

Kaminsky's IT Project Manager Framework

Kaminsky (2012) compared technical and nontechnical leadership practices in his study of IT project managers. This qualitative study was based on formal interviews with IT managers. The results identified many nontechnical behaviors that were necessary to solve problems in IT project teams. The study used Heifetz's adaptive leadership framework, which suggested that adaptive challenges are different from technical ones because they do not have straightforward solutions (Heifetz & Linsky, 2009). Rather, people in organizations must learn and change their attitudes, values, or behaviors rather than look to authority figures or clearly established systems to solve problems.

Kaminsky's (2012) study was one of the first academic research programs to examine nontechnical skills for IT project managers, and it was designed to test whether certain nontechnical skills in Heifetz's adaptive leadership framework were important for IT project managers' success. IT project managers of varying levels from three different organizations were asked what actions they took to solve certain kinds of challenges that typically arise for IT project managers. Two sets of skills emerged from the interviews. These were classified as technical and nontechnical, with nine skills in each category (see Exhibit 4.1). Several of the technical skills were well known in the field as best practices of project management with known technical solutions, such as scope and risk management. Technical skills also included HR management (e.g., staffing and training) and time management (e.g., prioritizing critical issues, using project metrics). Nontechnical skills included behaviors that were outside the scope of known project management best practices and were behaviors that matched ones on the nontechnical side of the adaptive leadership framework, such as anchoring oneself (e.g., venting, taking time away), going to the balcony

Exhibit 4.1	
Summary of Kaminsky (2012) Core Leadership Practices for Information Technology Project Managers	
Technical practices	Nontechnical practices
Integration management	Going to the balcony
Scope management	Identify the adaptive challenge
Time management	Cook the conflict and regulate distress
Cost management	Maintain disciplined attention
Quality management	Give work back to the people
Human resource management	Protect leadership below
Communications management	Take responsibility
Risk management	Hold steady
Procurement management	Anchor yourself

(mentally disengaging to gain perspective of the big picture), maintaining disciplined attention, taking responsibility, and driving change.

This model is intriguing because many practices that are often included in traditional HR leadership development models were classified as technical practices, such as communications management, time management, and even HR management. They were perceived as having systems, processes, and metrics, as well as authoritative solutions rather than interpersonal or intrapersonal ones. Kaminsky's model could be an effective one for consultants to use in coaching leaders on how to better manage teams. Getting the right communication systems in place, for example, is a technical solution that can be seen as more approachable than learning emotional intelligence. It may be a good place to start with leaders who are resistant to talking about psychological issues.

Some leadership skills do not lend themselves to step-by-step models, but they may be better received if they are presented as coming from a technical leader or model. For example, leadership concepts, such as introspection and vulnerability, are subtle and not easily conveyed using a step-by-step model. The nontechnical practices in Kaminsky's framework, such as finding a place of sanctuary to reflect and recharge to anchor oneself, are quite inward focused. If an organizational consultant made the suggestion to find a place of sanctuary to reflect, it might come across as foreign, but if it were quoted as something said by other IT project managers, it could be perceived quite differently. As described in Chapter 3, consultants can build credibility by using the words of the IT project managers, effectively speaking their language. By showing Kaminsky's nontechnical practices used by IT project managers to solve problems effectively, a consultant could break through a technical leader's resistance to change and help connect them with accessible behaviors to try to build their confidence and help them believe that it is possible.

Other Leadership Models That Appeal to Technical Leaders

In my experience, especially working with engineers, I have seen that once a technical leader decides they need to develop leadership skills, they tend to gravitate toward models, processes, and systems that have very specific steps, categories, and criteria to employ. I have seen technical leaders use such models as the radical candor model by Scott (2019), which categorizes performance feedback that a leader might give to someone into four quadrants—*ruinous empathy, manipulative insincerity, obnoxious aggression,* and *radical candor*—to help a leader understand how their feedback might come across to a recipient. A leader can use this simple test in the moment to identify and adjust their approach to giving feedback to make it more productive. Another example is Appelo's (2016) seven levels of delegation model, which is a quick check for a leader to use to determine how much to include or empower others in making a decision. The levels range from telling others that they have made the decision and why to delegating the decision to others entirely without wanting to know the details. Martino's (2018) five-step model for technical leaders to use in handling uncomfortable situations is another example. The five steps spell out the following sentence: Expect, understand, and own the positive future (p. 20). These models are not comprehensive, but they can be helpful tools for organizational consultants to recommend in the appropriate circumstances. See Table 3.1 for additional resources.

Educating and Training Tips for Technical Leaders

Technical leaders can benefit a great deal from interactive learning (Sansone & Schreiber-Abshire, 2011). One of my interview participants who was a VP of HR at a midsize publicly traded biotech company in Southern California suggested that leadership development for technical leaders was more effective when it is more interactive than didactic. Even simply giving them opportunities to compare notes and talk to each other was, in his experience, important. He said,

> At my current company, a lot of technical leaders are more introverted. They sit and listen. We have to push them to express themselves. However, it is one thing to listen and another to practice a skill. It is important to get them outside of their comfort zone. (Personal communication by an individual who did not wish to be cited by name, July 17, 2020)

This HR VP also noted that it is important not to take for granted that technical leaders will automatically understand the psychological parts of interaction. He continued,

> We get technical leaders who forget they are human and forget those elements exist. Technical leaders will often look at things in a factual way and not consider anything about feelings and impressions and context, or human behavioral issues. They don't always know what drives people to behave. We have to bring them along with the psychological aspects to help them allow for people space, and context. (Personal communication by an individual who did not wish to be cited by name, July 17, 2020)

Programs therefore may need to cover the basics and not make assumptions that basic social skills are in hand (Daniels, 2009; DeVilbiss & Gilbert, 2005; Kumar & Hsiao, 2007; Leonard, 2017; Sansone & Schreiber-Abshire, 2011). Phyllis Balan, another HR executive, recalled during her interview for this book,

> Recently, I was working with a couple of newer scientists and we sent them to a 1-day supervisory workshop, which was an introduction to

management. I was surprised to learn they had never seen any of the content before and it was foreign to them. After I thought about it, I realized the curriculum for scientists doesn't include any management theory. (P. Balan, personal communication, May 5, 2020)

Two things are key to appealing to technical leaders when introducing basic constructs. First is recognizing that they are smart, capable people. A trainer might say, "In your own fields you had to start from scratch and learn basic knowledge before you moved to the advanced parts, and that is exactly what we will be doing here." Second, programs should employ language that allows individuals to remain true to themselves while embracing new ways of thinking and behaving based on authentic leadership theory. For example, technical people tend to respond well to methods that help them "gather data" to use in their decision making, such as identifying situations that trigger frustration. Consultants might call this "building self-awareness." Technical people may also be dubious of the idea of talking about "emotions," but they usually are less trepidatious when the language is changed to discussing what their "reactions" are.

Following the SERC example, programs should differ depending on the leadership level. Examples of topics for team and first-level leaders include expanding the scientific black-and-white mindset to incorporate emotions into awareness, developing empathy, and communication skills to influence team members and cross-functional peers and others inside and outside of the organization. As leaders progress into higher levels, the focus should shift to business acumen, managing up, and big-picture thinking.

Two Contrasting Examples for Developing Leaders

Before Adriana Cabre moved into the life-sciences industry, she spent over a decade in HR at a Fortune 100 high-tech company. When I interviewed her for this book, Ms. Cabre (personal communication, April 17, 2020) explained the first-time-manager training that had been developed at the company. Managers who went through the program had to have regular refresher courses consisting of at least 4 hours per year. They had separate management training sessions for first-time managers, for technical managers, and for middle managers. They also had training for technical managers that focused on the nontechnical parts. They created an individual-contributor (IC) leadership ladder to avoid losing talented engineers because they were not "people people." She said that they had lost people at the high-tech company because they put "a square peg in round hole." It was not the right job for them.

Ms. Cabre contrasted her work at the high-tech company with her experiences developing and deploying training for technical leaders in life-sciences companies. The company goal for one pharmaceutical company was to learn how to spot the scientists and technical writers who had "the people factor." The company started a program for emerging leaders and gave them opportunities to lead two or three people as a "lead" but not yet as a formal direct manager. These people still reported to a manager, but the day-to-day actions were directed by the lead. She observed that no one completed all the trainings, but those who participated in the program said it was transformational. The training focused a lot on them getting to know themselves, then getting to know their teams and how to interact better. She said that some opted out of the program and relinquished their management positions along the way. They found it to be "50% more headaches for 10% more salary." The energy and stress depleted them so much. They put them instead on the IC ladder with no supervisory responsibilities. Ms. Cabre said, "We had so many talented people who were doing so much work, and we were going to lose them if we didn't promote them."

At the pharmaceutical company, half of the participants opted out. Although the engineers at the high-tech company complied and did their 4 hours per year, at the pharmaceutical company, it was different. "The FDA can tell the scientists to comply, but HR cannot," Ms. Cabre said. She also explained that many scientists said they did not want to do an upcoming leadership program because they did not have the time, but it was also clear some were not comfortable managing and telling people what to do and questioning their work. She surmised that "they simply did not want to do it; the demand outweighed the reward."

DIVERSITY CHALLENGES FOR INDIVIDUAL TECHNICAL LEADERS

Because STEM (science, technology, engineering, and mathematics) industries tend to have less diversity on a number of dimensions than do other industries, consultants may find that issues of diversity and inclusion surface in their work with technical leaders. This section describes the diversity landscape in STEM, specific challenges that arise for technical leaders, and suggestions for consulting to them on these issues at the individual level. Diversity is addressed at the group and organizational levels in subsequent chapters.

Diversity Landscape in STEM

According to a report from the National Science Foundation, women made up 29% of the workforce in science and engineering in 2017 (Khan et al., 2020). The Pew Research Center analyzed data from the U.S. Census Bureau from 1990 to 2017 and found that the share of women working in STEM occupations remained at roughly 50% when health care workers were included (Funk & Parker, 2018). The percentage varied across industry and job, however. Many more women were in health care than in engineering, for example. Women made up about 14% of engineers, 25% of computer scientists (a decrease from 32% in 1990), 90% of nurses, and 96% of speech language pathologists (Funk & Parker, 2018; Kaiser Family Foundation, 2020). Research has also shown that, although the majority of health care workers are women, women are underrepresented in research science and in leadership roles in academic medicine and better paid medical specialties, like surgery (Coe et al., 2019). When health care is removed from STEM and the U.S. Bureau of Labor Statistics definition is used, women make up only 26% of the STEM workforce (U.S. Department of Labor, 2018).

When coaching individual technical leaders, organizational consultants may find that different challenges arise for women than for men. For example, with the low numbers of women in STEM occupations, women often have few role models and may lack mentors, sponsors, and confidantes. Men, being the majority, may be unaware of these unique challenges, or they may be looking for guidance on how to help.

The women whom I interviewed for this book tended to describe different experiences as technical leaders than did the men. Although some of their experiences were positive and some negative, all respondents, including the men, said the percentages of women in their fields were very low. A chemical engineer who moved to software development said that the field of chemical engineering was 50% women when she graduated from her doctoral program but when she moved into software development, it was "so much more male dominated" (personal communication by an individual who did not wish to be cited by name, April 10, 2020). She said she was surprised and ill prepared. She expressed her frustration with frequently being interrupted and minimized. She said she was often "mansplained" by engineers in her company and by clients, meaning that people, particularly men, explained things to her that she already knew in a condescending or patronizing way. She said cultural differences were at play, with men from some cultures being a lot less open to women in engineering than others are. Another woman said,

> I get this on a regular basis: "You're very assertive, and you're hard to deal with because of your communication style of being direct." If you're male, people say you're very direct and you get things done. If you're female, they say you're bitchy. I have to present questions in a different way than I normally would because I have to deal with men who are older. Men my own age like me and deal well with my approach. There is a generation gap. (Personal communication by an individual who did not wish to be cited by name, June 8, 2020)

White and Asian American people are overrepresented in the STEM workforce, whereas Black and Hispanic American people are underrepresented, compared with the proportions in the general U.S. workforce (Funk & Parker, 2018). For example, 9% of STEM workers are Black people, and 7% are Hispanic people, but the groups represent 11% and 16% of the U.S. workforce, respectively. As with gender, organizational consultants may want to prepare themselves to coach on unique challenges for technical leaders in minority racial groups.

Diversity has not substantially increased in STEM between 2000 and 2020, especially for women and lesbian, gay, bisexual, transgender, and questioning or queer and others, African American, and Latino people (Bidwell, 2015; Dutt, 2018). Many explanations for these findings are offered in the news and research, including both explicit and implicit bias, lack of empathy, socioeconomic factors (such as the length and expense of training needed to attain many STEM jobs), and self-selection (Dutt, 2018; Fiske et al., 2010; Gavet, 2021; Hiltzik, 2018). In the interviews conducted for this book, technical leaders, organizational consultants, and HR leaders had mixed observations of how diversity was approached in technical industries. They noted that concern with diversity varied depended largely on organizations' size and values. The technical leaders and consultants often observed that the reason for lack of diversity among technical organizations was simply lack of time and attention to the matter. Others found their organizations to already be quite diverse, either by coincidence or by design.

Consulting to Technical Leaders at the Individual Level on Diversity and Inclusion

Sometimes consultants are asked to coach technical leaders specifically on diversity and inclusion issues, and sometimes these issues may arise in the consultant's assessment. As shown in the consulting model in Figure 3.2, two major challenges that arise when consulting to technical leaders are specific types of resistance and disconnect. As described in previous chapters, the disconnect factor, or unawareness, stems from the fact that technical leaders tend to be very focused on delivering results on their projects and may be less aware of big-picture issues. They also tend to be extremely busy people who are in critical functions for their organizations. Not only may technical leaders be unaware or unconcerned about diversity issues, but they may resist efforts to increase diversity either because they are skeptical and do not see the evidence to support the value of the effort or because they may not see evidence that they are indeed not supporting diversity.

Inclusive leadership can be a tall order for some technical leaders. Inclusive leadership requires a level of awareness to see people's identities and figure out the differences that matter (Ferdman, 2021). It requires leaders to be interpersonally skilled to provide "space and perspectives to help people recognize, appreciate, address, and work with these differences in a positive way" (Ferdman, 2021, p. 8). It also requires courage and tact to be able to challenge harmful biases and discriminatory beliefs and behaviors. Technical leaders who are overworked, who are laser focused on meeting their project goals, who approach interpersonal interactions in a transactional way, who lack empathy, who see things categorically, who are trained to defend their position vehemently, and/or who need data to support every assertion will likely miss cues, make people feel unsafe, and perpetuate biases and discrimination, perhaps completely unwittingly.

Organizational consultants can also help technical leaders be more inclusive by bringing group differences to their awareness. Many tools can be employed to increase self- and other awareness. For example, there are tools to increase cognitive and social agility (see Bradberry & Greaves, 2009; Jøsok et al., 2019, for examples) and tools for technical leaders to explore their values and leadership principles (see George, 2015, for examples). Once leaders are more aware of themselves and others, consultants can continue to use these tools and others to help leaders learn how to create psychological safety or safe spaces to have authentic conversations with their teams (American Psychological Association, 2019; Ferdman et al., 2021; Google, 2020a; Patterson et al., 2002).

SUMMARY

During individual consulting engagements, consultants may find they connect better with their technical clients when they shift their methods and mindsets to match those of their clients. Characteristically technical experts at their core, these leaders often have not had extensive training on the interpersonal side of leadership, and they may not value it as much as others do. Several examples in this chapter illustrate how consultants can anticipate and work through prototypical forms of resistance from technical leaders and bridge the gap between psychological and technical ways of thinking. Consultants may also find it useful to employ leadership models specifically designed for technical leaders. The chapter includes several examples of well-researched models that contain both technical and nontechnical behaviors and that use language that may appeal to technical leaders.

In addition to understanding how technical leaders think and the specific skills that are valuable for them to develop, consultants who understand the context in which technical leaders work may find it easier to make headway with their clients. One contextual factor was raised in this chapter, the lack of diversity in STEM, but other industry characteristics, such as design methodologies and regulatory requirements, also influence how technical leaders operate. The following chapters give more context into technical teams and organizations that will help consultants work with technical leaders at any level of consulting—individual, group, or organizational.

5

Consulting at the Group Level: Understanding Technical Teams

In this chapter, the focus moves from the individual to the group level. I describe the characteristics that technical teams have in common with other teams; some of their differentiating features, including environmental influences; and five typical characteristics of technical teams, along with some of their challenges. The chapter includes suggestions and resources for addressing these issues, as well as descriptions of specific team frameworks and regulatory constraints that commonly determine the context in which technical teams function, such as Agile and Scrum methodologies (Stellman & Greene, 2013), the FDA approval process mandated for drug and biotech companies, and compliance with standards relevant to other areas of STEM (science, technology, engineering, and mathematics). Glossaries for important terminology used in life sciences and Agile teams are in Tables 5.1 and 5.2, respectively. Resources for further reading on some of the most common technical team contexts are provided.

https://doi.org/10.1037/0000270-006
Consulting to Technical Leaders, Teams, and Organizations: Building Leadership in STEM Environments, by J. B. Connell

Table 5.1

Life Sciences and Health Care Drug and Device Development: Glossary of U.S. Food and Drug Administration (FDA) Terminology

Term	Definition/usage
Discovery	Researchers seek to understand the disease to be treated and its surrounding context and systematically reverse-engineer treatments.
Target	A molecule in the body, typically a protein, that is associated with a particular disease and that could be addressed by a drug to produce a desired therapeutic result. During the first phase of drug discovery, scientists must understand the molecular basis of a disease to find targets.
Screen	Scientists screen chemical libraries of small molecules to identify compounds that effectively (with high affinity) bind to the target.
Assay	A system created by scientists to test the effects of chemical compounds on a cellular, molecular, or biochemical process.
Hit	A promising compound from an assay screening.
Lead	Hits are examined further to find the best of them, which are called leads. Leads are the starting points for drug development.
Preclinical research	Testing a drug candidate in the lab or on animals before it is tested on humans.
In vitro	A process of testing in test tubes, using more assays.
In vivo	A process of testing in living organisms, such as animals.
IND	Investigational new drug (IND) application for FDA approval to move to clinical testing.
Clinical research	Three highly regulated phases of human testing.
Pharmacokinetics	Effects of a therapeutic on the body, such as absorption, metabolic, elimination, and side effects.
NDA, ANDA, BLA	The FDA review starts when researchers prepare an application for approval of the drug in a new drug application (NDA) or abbreviated new drug application (ANDA) or biologics license application (BLA).

Table 5.2
Software Development and Engineering: **Glossary of Agile Terminology**

Term	Definition
Waterfall methodology	A design methodology that dates back to the 1950s and came out of the manufacturing industry. Projects are planned up front from beginning to end as a series of successive development phases that start with documenting specifications, continue with developing, then testing, and so on, until the product is released to the customer (Royce, 1970). The downsides are that many sequential dependencies affect quality and time to delivery and that the customer does not receive anything until the product is complete.
Agile	A project management philosophy that utilizes a core set of values or principles. Organizations implement Agile using one or a combination of frameworks, such as Scrum and Kanban. The philosophy infers a process that is more efficient and responsive to changing customer demands and that produces higher quality results in a timelier fashion than the waterfall method. Embedded in this philosophy is delivering usable code to customers quickly and adding features and resolving problems along the way (Beck et al., 2001; Stellman & Greene, 2013).
Agile team	A team that follows the Agile philosophy and typically adheres to one or parts of several Agile frameworks.
Common Agile frameworks	Scrum and Kanban are the two most popular, but others include Extreme Programming (XP), Feature-Driven Development (FDD), Adaptive System Development (ASD), Dynamic Systems Development Method (DSDM), Lean Software Development (LSD), and Crystal Clear (Eby, 2017).
Scrum	A software development framework that focuses on optimizing predictability and controlling risk by using a repeated incremental approach that includes regular team check-ins and customer feedback. Teams are autonomous, self-organized, and cross-functional.
Kanban	A visual framework that came out of the Toyota Production System and Lean Manufacturing philosophies. *Kanban* is Japanese for "visual sign" or "card." Similar to how store clerks restock shelves when they notice they are empty, software development teams can restock their workload by showing visual cues to others when they have work capacity.
Sprint	A scrum development cycle, typically 2 to 6 weeks long. A large project is broken down into smaller chunks, called sprints. At the end of each sprint, software is delivered to the customer.

(continues)

Table 5.2
Software Development and Engineering:
Glossary of Agile Terminology (*Continued*)

Term	Definition
Stand-up meeting	In a scrum framework, a daily meeting in which the entire team is present in a room, face to face and standing to reinforce that the meeting should be short, as in 15 minutes.
Retrospective meeting (retro)	A team meeting at the end of a sprint to take inventory of what went well and what did not go well during the sprint; the team focuses on a number of different dimensions, including teamwork.
Scrum master	Person who manages the process of the Scrum team.
Project owner	Person who manages the entire project and plans sprints with the Scrum master.
Backlog	List of tasks that need to be completed for a project.

Group-level diversity and inclusion, global and virtual teams, and other team issues are also addressed. I begin the chapter with a case example of a pharmaceutical research and development (R&D) team to illustrate some common issues that arise in consulting engagements with technical teams in general and drug development teams in particular.

CASE EXAMPLE: AN UNCOOPERATIVE PHARMACEUTICAL DEVELOPMENT TEAM

The chief human resources (HR) officer of a small medical device company brought in an organizational consultant to assess and develop the team consisting of vice presidents and executive directors (i.e., just below the C-Suite). The leaders would likely be equivalent to directors at a larger company in leadership responsibilities, even though many of these leaders had had no leadership experience outside of this company or academia. The VP of HR explained to the consultant that the team experienced a lot of turbulence, that they were not communicating with each other and were working in silos, and that one of the members of the board of directors had approached her with concerns that the team may not be able to grow the company. They were developing a device that would allow doctors to test patients in the office for the presence of certain cancers instead of having to send samples out to a lab. The upside potential for the company was huge.

Initial interviews with the team members provided only faint indications of what the VP of HR had reported to the consultant. Roger was in charge of the life cycle management of the product; he managed the process planning to take the product through the phases of development to manufacturing. He had no aspirations for promotion in the near future and was content in his current role. He downplayed the conflicts on the team, saying the others were pretty young and inexperienced in industry and had a lot of maturing to do.

Hiram oversaw preclinical development. His teams presided over activities that linked the device development in the laboratory to initiation of human clinical trials. This was his first industry job out of academia, and he saw himself eventually being the chief science officer (CSO). He had been at the company the longest and was frustrated because, as the company grew and his decision-making power diminished, he felt that he was constantly being demoted. His resentment was apparent in his demeanor as he spoke. He was subtle in his criticisms of others and complained about others not sharing information and trying to take ownership of work that he saw as his.

Renee was in charge of data analysis for commercialization, and she was "no nonsense" in her approach to others. She did not engage in small talk and even said outright that she had no interest in learning about people's personal lives or in sharing anything about hers. She explained how incompetent the others on the team were and how she frequently had to argue with them to keep them from trying to take her work away from her. She also said that the clinical and process development groups were constantly at each other's throats.

Sabina oversaw building out the quality control team and had only one direct report at the time. She was new to the organization, had several years of experience at a large pharmaceutical company, and had high hopes for cooperation from her teammates.

Raj, the CSO, had supported the idea of bringing in the consultant for team building but found excuses not to be included in the activities himself. He attended the first team-building session and afterward said he was delighted to see how much it helped his team work together. He kept supporting the consultant's efforts and agreeing to take part, but when the time arose either to complete self-assessments or to attend coaching or team-building meetings, he did not follow through. The consultant raised the issue of his lack of participation, and he said he would make more of an effort, but he kept getting pulled away on "more important" tasks, such as presenting to the board of directors or to the FDA. The team went through a 360-degree feedback process, which provided useful information to the individual targets and to the team as a whole. However, most team members were resistant to the feedback, rationalized their low scores, and did not make serious attempts to change their behavior. The team-building program kept getting postponed because the team had important projects and meetings, and it dragged on for 6 months without much progress.

Among the challenges for a consultant working with a life sciences team are to follow and understand highly technical information they are speaking about in their meetings and to be able to respond in their language and ask further questions about the issues raised. This case study was written for an organizational consultant to understand it. The way the directors spoke during the interviews, however, was almost in a different language. Responses often sounded more like "I lead the R&D team in the implementation of the LIFSVR assay for treatment response monitoring in oncological diseases and set up contract manufacturing for IVD assays," "We had developed a robust and technically challenging DNA assay to visualize replication at the level of the single molecule," and "The ASR wasn't getting the results we wanted." The following sections of this chapter provide some relevant vocabulary to help organizational consultants understand the contexts of technical teams in STEM industries.

Another challenge is to figure out the interpersonal dynamics within the team when the team members do not talk about them. Clearly this is a challenge with any team, but as I explained in Chapter 4, technical people often display certain types of resistance and disconnect. Technical team members are often less aware of the people dynamics, and it can almost feel like an interrogation to get them to provide information about how people work together (Chen & Simpson, 2015; Jack et al., 2013; Rasoal et al., 2012). They may also be less interested in talking about these matters, feeling that it is a distraction from the work they have to complete on urgent deadlines. They may simply be uncomfortable talking about these issues. It can take a lot of creativity on the part of the consultant to find the right questions to ask to get them talking about the team's dynamics. As discussed in Chapter 4, it is up to the consultant to resolve the resistance and dissolve the disconnect.

Raj, the CSO, was resisting leadership development. It later surfaced that he had thought that receiving coaching was punitive; in fact, he perceived it as a masked message from the CEO that he was failing, rather than an attempt to help him and his team be more successful. Raj was one of the five original members of the company. The original members were friends from graduate school, and the product came out of the CEO's dissertation research. Raj had never worked in industry, led a team, or participated in any leadership training before joining the company. He now had more than 90 people working for him. After 6 months of trying to engage Raj in development, the exasperated consultant had a check-in meeting with the VP of HR, who reported that Raj had finally agreed to have coaching. It was shortly after that meeting that the team building actually began. The team needed his sponsorship to take it seriously, and over the next 6 months they made a dramatic turnaround with the help of team building. Through intense conversation and honest feedback in a safe team-building environment, they learned how to trust and support each other and to show alignment in front of their teams. Their progress was so dramatic that the C-Suite decided to get coaches and introduce team building to their team as well.

COMMON CHARACTERISTICS AND CHALLENGES OF TECHNICAL TEAMS

This case example illustrates some of the challenges that arise in technical teams. In this section, I describe several common characteristics of technical teams and the challenges that can emerge from these characteristics. First, however, I identify characteristics common to all groups or teams.

In many ways, technical teams and groups are like all groups. As Mathieu et al. (2017) described, teams consist of two or more people, they have a purpose, they require interaction of their members in support of common goals, and they all have leadership functions. There are formal and informal roles within all groups, and groups and teams in organizations work within a larger organization that typically includes many other teams. Most groups also have conflict both within the team and with other groups in the organization (DeVilbiss & Gilbert, 2005; Vieth & Smith, 2008).

What's Distinctive About Technical Teams?

Many technical teams have certain distinctive, differentiating features. For example, leadership roles in technical teams are often less straightforward due to matrixed organizations, in which employees may work on multiple teams and report to the same or different managers than those on their teams, and the goals tend to change very quickly so that alignment between leaders and teams can be particularly challenging (BlessingWhite, 2013). In addition, specific contexts in which technical teams work can be quite distinctive and control behavior. Engineers, for example, are increasingly using Agile team methodology to direct the way they operate; pharmaceutical teams must follow highly regulated FDA R&D procedures; and physicians work in highly structured roles and must follow privacy laws, health insurance mandates, and professional licensing protocols. It is useful for a consultant to have some knowledge of the specific technical context when working with such teams (Berman, 2019; Walker, 2019). The challenges are outlined in Table 5.3, and the details are explained in the following sections.

Setting Goals of Innovation Versus Results

Technical managers may run into conflicts as they structure goals and measure progress of work completed by the team. The organizational leadership may want innovation, especially in technical organizations, but they invariably want results too. If both are required from the same team,

Table 5.3

Five Characteristics of Technical Teams

Characteristic	Explanation	Challenges
Innovative and/or results driven	Research and development have different outcomes. Research produces new ideas, and development implements them.	Ambiguous performance goals
Different personalities	Creative innovators may clash with disciplined scientists in their values and the way they work.	Conflicting work styles
Rapid change	Competition, customers, success, and failure all can instantaneously change what needs to be done.	Speed and flexibility
Multidisciplinary	People from multiple disciplines are needed to solve a problem or build something. Multiple disciplines can be within a team as well as across functions in the organization.	Communication and collaboration
Specific framework	Different industries have different method-ologies and contexts that teams must follow, such as Agile, FDA, IRS, and academic frameworks.	Defining and maintaining roles and responsibilities

Note. Information is from participant responses in the interview study of technical leaders, organizational consultants, and human resources leaders conducted for this book. FDA = U.S. Food and Drug Administration; IRS = Internal Revenue Service.

performance goals can be ambiguous. Should the manager allocate time for team members to generate ideas? Should the manager give leeway to employees to let creativity work on its own schedule? Should they set rigid timelines for projects to be completed no matter what? Should the team follow a systematic process for development? Should the organization reward the team for innovation or for results? Not only do these two different goals create ambiguous expectations for performance, but they can also lead to friction among team members as well as challenges to carrying out fair reward structures.

For example, 2-week Agile sprints and other tightly scheduled work deadlines may be great for producing results but are not necessarily conducive to creative exploration or filling the need for some creative people to play and experiment. Mari Casserberg is an IT leader for a privately owned software company that has about 600 employees. When I asked her what was missing from technical leadership, she responded,

> There is not enough time for invention and creativity. People are working on the problem statement that's given to them. There is very little tinkering time left to explore outside the customer deliverable they're working on. Everyone is very laser focused. (M. Casserberg, personal communication, April 10, 2020)

Some technical leaders build what they call "creative time" for their developers within sprints. A developer may, for example, be allowed 4 hours of time to tinker around on an unrelated project during the sprint.

Organizational consultants and HR leaders can help managers of technical teams develop processes to incentivize and measure creativity, innovation, and results. McKay and colleagues' (2020) book, *Creative Success in Teams*, is a good resource for research-backed methods to build diverse teams that lend themselves to creative problem solving, motivating team members to be creative, establishing environments in which team members freely exchange ideas, and structuring procedures to maximize team innovation. Consultants can also help diverse teams increase trust and communication to encourage creativity and reduce conflict (DeVilbiss & Gilbert, 2005; McKay et al., 2020).

Managing Conflicting Personalities in Technical Teams

Personality conflicts can be a challenge for any group, but certain tensions may arise in technical teams because of the nature of the work and the characteristics of the people who tend to do the work. For example, innovation is a key component of many technical organizations, and being innovative differentiates the top companies in the world from the rest (Ringel et al., 2020). Innovation comes in different forms. Spontaneous, unconscious creativity is a much different process from disciplined experimentation (Dietrich, 2004). Thomas Edison was a disciplined innovator. One of his less famous quotes is "I never did anything by accident, nor did any of my inventions come by accident; they came by work." This is the way drug therapies are most often developed. It is a methodical process of weeding out tens of thousands of failures. Innovation can also come out of an accumulation of small systematic advances, such as the way computers were developed (Isaacson, 2014).

On the other hand, some inventors are imaginative people who see beauty and make connections that others do not see between seemingly unrelated things (Sato, 2016). Steve Jobs was this type of creative thinker. This kind of thinking is rare, and it does not work on a schedule (Sternberg, 1999). The combination of spontaneous, emotionally driven creative people working with cognitively driven, disciplined personalities can result in frustration among the team members. As a result, the team members may adhere to different values, use different processes, and work on different timelines. Organizational consultants can help teams organize roles that match individual styles, foster an inclusive environment to appreciate differences, select a mix of personalities complementary on multiple dimensions, incentivize team members to share knowledge, create workflow processes that allow for autonomy, and work toward appropriate goals (Sousa & Luís, 2013). In addition to getting the team members to work well with each other, the manager who demands innovation must appreciate creative personalities who may be rebellious and nonconforming and support an environment of creativity (Jauk et al., 2019; Sato, 2016).

The Impact of Rapid Change on Technical Teams

In a rapidly moving field involving technology, teams often need to be able to change direction quickly. A single tweet, a new app, or news from across the world can change everything in a matter of days. In Chapter 2, I provided many examples of leaders describing rapid change with which they had to keep up. Demands for rapid change also affect groups. Teams have to be flexible in order to be able to change directions and to stop and start new projects. Reasons for sudden changes include the customers wanting something different from what they originally requested, the competition beating the company's product to market, the product the company is creating does not work, or something else, such as new technology, disrupting the industry (Roth, 2020; Stellman & Greene, 2013).

Productive group processes, such as the four stages of team development (i.e., forming, storming, norming, performing; Tuckman, 1965), can be challenged by the need for rapid change. A team that keeps changing because of fast growth, high turnover, or shifting project requirements might get stuck in forming, repeating the cycle of orienting themselves to each other and testing the boundaries. If stuck in the stage of storming, they might resist group influence and task requirements, and if stuck at or before norming, they might never develop cohesion or make it to the performing stage of team development, when they would be functioning optimally.

One pharmaceutical team I worked with had three managers within a 1-year time span because of turnover and reorganization at the company. Every time a new leader arrived, there was a new shuffle of the roles and responsibilities of the team members. After a year of constant change, the team members were so unclear about the team members' roles (and their own) that they became embroiled in classic team dysfunction (Lencioni, 2002). Although the team members were highly capable and conscientious as individuals, they had lost confidence that each other's intentions were good, and they became protective and cautious when interacting with one another, at the expense of the team's dynamics and productivity. They needed a period of stability to get the trust back on track, including 6 months of team-building interventions that focused on engaging in constructive dialogue and developing decision-making processes and accountability metrics.

In Raj's team, presented in the case example at the beginning of this chapter, the R&D division had undergone several restructures during the company's period of rapid growth. At one point, the lines of accountability were blurred, they had failed an FDA inspection, and the company received a warning letter from the FDA for failure to provide adequate accountability and disposition records for the investigational product. The problems were rectified immediately, but the reputation of the research team had been tarnished, and some of the other leaders in the company no longer trusted the team. For his part, Raj had been so focused on the details of the technology he had not noticed the lack of communication among members of the team.

One way organizational consultants can help rapidly growing teams is by offering them the three rapid-growth leadership steps of awareness, systems, and accountability, shown in Figure 5.1. The first step (i.e., awareness) begins with the team leader, but it also applies to the entire team. As I described in Chapters 1 and 2, technical people tend to be so focused on meeting project goals they may be unaware of dysfunctional team dynamics. I illustrated two factors, resistance and disconnect, that tend to arise when consulting to technical leaders in the model shown in Figure 3.2. These factors work at the team level as well. Technical leaders and team members may need to overcome their disconnect and become aware that the team has grown to a point at which they need systems and accountability as well as potentially new roles, processes, and people (Kendra & Taplin, 2004). Then the leader and team members may need to work through their own resistance to both (a) having to step out of the science and into the leadership role and (b) bogging the team down with systems for tracking progress. The attitude that systems are cumbersome rather than desirable is common in fast-growing organizations, especially for entrepreneurial leaders who prefer a hands-on, flexible approach (Frese & Gielnik, 2014). Usually, leaders and team members need to feel a bit of pain before they are ready to embrace the change.

In the second step of the rapid-growth leadership model (i.e., systems), leaders need to establish a project management system to track roles, resources, time, and so on. The consultant may suggest process management methods like Appelo's (2016) seven levels of delegation model for

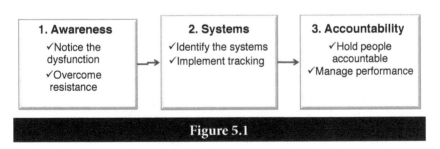

Figure 5.1

Steps for a rapid-growth leadership intervention.

defining how decisions are made in teams, the Belbin® Team Roles model for dividing the work into different types of actions, or Agile or Scrum frameworks to clarify timing and process of the work. Additionally, the consultant may suggest project management tools, such as Gantt charts and project workflow diagrams that are frequently employed in scientific teams to schedule different components of the work (Van den Berg & Pietersma, 2014).

In the third step (i.e., accountability), leaders need to hold team members accountable for their responsibilities. This process involves tracking and performance management. Tracking may come more easily for methodically oriented leaders; it is the performance management in which the consultant can typically help the most. A consultant may offer the leader coaching on how to deliver feedback, having uncomfortable conversations, the importance of one-on-one meetings, and so on.

Complex Team Structures Cause Ambiguous Leadership

Modern technical teams are typically multidisciplinary and matrixed. This structure can encourage streamlined results, quick responses to rapid change, innovation, and ability to serve external stakeholders, such as customers and collaborators. A VP of R&D for a technology company explained in their interview for this book, "Team leadership is typically project based. A team leader is selected to lead a small group of technical employees that are working on the same project" (personal communication by an individual who did not wish to be cited by name, May 1, 2020).

One of the challenges with multidisciplinary teams is ambiguous leadership (BlessingWhite, 2013). In other words, team members and leaders themselves are not necessarily clear on the responsibilities and authority that the leaders have because multiple leaders are usually involved in projects. Project leaders often do not have personnel responsibilities for their team members and, when they do, they may not have a deep enough understanding of what team members from other disciplines do to evaluate their performance effectively. Sarah Moran described her experience leading development teams that follow the Agile philosophy (described in the next section of this chapter):

> With Agile, you end up getting a matrix of leadership involved in everything. One person leads the team in terms of work, but people don't report to them. They report to people in a particular domain. It's the necessity of interfacing with a lot of stakeholders and partners. Alignment and agreement across leaders are necessary for it to work. (S. Moran, personal communication, April 14, 2020)

Regardless of whether Agile is employed, small and large technical organizations may have ambiguous leadership for different reasons. A large pharma company, for example, might have grown to include multiple levels of hierarchy that include different geographical, therapy, and functional areas, resulting in slow decision making, poor communication, and divisive politics (Kleinman, 2017). A start-up biotech firm, in contrast, may be a leaner, less hierarchical organization, but team members may not know who is the decision maker on issues because the leadership roles overlap and the leaders have their hands in multiple domains. Areas in which organizational consultants can help are improving communication and empathy among technical teams, relationship building, and influencing to build alignment and intergroup relationships (Hogg et al., 2012; Kendra & Taplin, 2004; Pandya, 2014).

Technical Teams May Use Specific Design Methodologies and Frameworks

One of the biggest challenges for organizational consultants working with technical organizations is to understand the context in which technical teams work. Technical industries tend to use specific team frameworks and work with certain regulating bodies that dictate the processes they must follow. In the pharmaceutical team scenario presented above, for example, the team was working in the context of a tightly controlled, highly complex and legalistic FDA development framework. The FDA has specific phases of research that must be followed so that the product being developed is compliant with the regulations governing whether the drug will ultimately be approved for sale, and different teams are often created to address each phase (see Table 5.1 for explanations of these phases and definitions of other important terms related to the FDA drug approval process).

Tech development teams tend to use the Agile framework or derivatives of it that call for highly structured back-to-back rapid design cycles in which team members meet daily, have tight deadlines, and work continuously, without breaks, to frequently deliver value to customers (Denning, 2018; Rigby et al., 2016; Stellman & Greene, 2013; see Table 5.2 for explanations of basic Agile terminology). Additionally, scientific research tends to be based on an academic framework whether or not the work is housed in a university (Khan et al., 2020). Funding and peer reviewed journals have very specific requirements, and institutes are set up to generate results that will pass muster in journals and research grant proposals.

Frameworks challenge both the consultant and the technical teams. Although the goal of employing frameworks is to make roles and responsibilities more clear-cut, frameworks can also increase complexity and ambiguity. The following sections describe the most common frameworks and areas in which organizational consultants can help.

Software Development: The Agile Framework

In 2001, a group of 17 developers joined forces to establish a better way of developing software, which they named the Agile method and published openly online in what they called the *Manifesto for Agile Software Development* (Beck et al., 2001). Their goal was to bring about a process that was efficient and responsive to changing customer demands and that produced high-quality results in a timely fashion. Embedded in this philosophy is delivering usable code to customers quickly and adding features and resolving problems along the way. Agile caught on quickly, and most companies use some form of Agile in their software development teams. Organizations implement Agile using one or a combination of frameworks, such as Scrum and Kanban. These frameworks are briefly described along with a number of other Agile terms in Table 5.2. Many books describe the Agile methodology, but one of the best is Stellman and Greene's (2013) *Learning Agile*. It is useful for organizational consultants to understand a little bit about the context of Agile and what the philosophy is to consult to software development teams who employ it.

What Does Agile Mean to Organizational Consultants?

Agile is a contemporary software development methodology that was created to make development teams more efficient and better serve customers. It does this by breaking down projects into small pieces, structuring team processes, empowering the teams, and including people outside of development on the teams. There are a lot of places where organizational consultants can help them.

First, although Agile emphasizes efficiency, it incurs a lot of overhead. The Agile team has long planning meetings and retrospectives every couple of weeks. Agile teams have limited management involvement, but people on the teams, such as the scrum master and the project owner, lead the projects. Agile teams use the quality and quantity of working code as metrics to demonstrate they are effective, but other measures that might be considered are often ignored. Organizational consultants may be able to help with efficiency in other domains, such as business and intra- and interteam dynamics. Some of these measures are part of the process, but they are not necessarily tracked in terms of success, and they are often the areas in which the teams struggle.

There are many kinds of process-based coaches and consultants who generally help teams improve by employing a specific methodology. For example, Lean Six Sigma consultants have been helping teams become more efficient since the 1980s (Socconini & Reato, 2018). Agile coaches help teams use the Agile process. Agile consultants tend to have technical backgrounds, not psychological backgrounds, and they tend to stick to the Agile methodology. In fact, their goal is primarily to coach individuals and teams on how to use Agile better to achieve a higher level of performance (Adkins, 2010). Agile is most successful when teams adhere strictly to the Agile principles and methodologies, and it takes courageous, vigilant leaders to keep the teams and organizational management on track (Denning, 2018). At the same time, teams are teams, and dysfunction may exist in Agile teams as in any other teams. Some Agile coaches focus on improving team dynamics, but they may be limited by having only software development backgrounds and no psychological training (Bäcklander, 2019). As such, there is room for organizational consultants to complement or partner with Agile consultants and even to become certified in one of the Agile frameworks. Many organizations certify coaches and consultants in their specific processes using their specific tools to implement various Agile frameworks.

Second, Agile teams work in fast-paced self-managed sprints that, as a primary rule, are not to be interrupted for anything or by anyone. This process leaves little room for coaching and consulting. As Adkins (2010) described, Agile coaches are taught to coach the team at the beginning and end of the sprints during their planning and retrospective meetings. They are taught to coach individuals only as absolutely necessary during the sprints and to leave as much as possible to the retrospective meetings. For organizational consultants to be welcomed and effective, coaching and consulting must be extremely efficient, time bound, and applied without disrupting the team's work. Short coaching sessions, brief engagements, and team building in between sprints are all suggestions for working with Agile teams.

Third, Agile teams are supposed to be autonomous and self-managed. Their success depends on team members being capable, motivated, and cooperative (Rigby et al., 2016). Therefore, it is critical to hire the right people—ones who can get along with each other, communicate across functions, self-reflect, and give and take feedback. Technical organizations do not typically focus on these skills in their hiring process. Rather, they focus heavily on technical skills and abilities. They are concerned about what is often referred to as *tech debt* (i.e., the cost of maintaining and reworking code because shortcuts were taken during development) but do not see how their hiring and people-management practices incur what I call *team debt* (i.e., the cost of maintaining and replacing team members because shortcuts were taken during hiring).

Fourth, one of the limitations with using the Agile framework is that it is based on a number of assumptions, such as the idea that people on the team trust each other, communicate well, and deliver honest feedback.

It also assumes the team will stick to a strict Agile process. Most teams do not strictly adhere to the Agile philosophy, and most team members suffer from the usual conditions of being human. In other words, there is a lot of room for team development in the areas of communication and trust. This area is one in which organizational consultants may be able to help the most. Organizational consultants can also help teams at a higher level. Agile team leaders do not usually have people-management responsibilities, only team-leadership responsibilities. Software development companies have managers and executives who deal with the people side of things and who set the project goals and allocate resources to the teams. Organizational consultants, particularly leadership coaches, can help managers to develop people-management skills, understand how to support their teams, and improve cross-functional communication.

Finally, the Agile methodology is not limited to software development (Denning, 2018). The Business Agility movement, for example, began in 2009 and extends Agile principles to the field of business analysis. The Agile Alliance (https://www.agilealliance.org/) is a good resource to learn more about the application of Agile principles to the field of business. Agile has also made a dent into science, construction, and manufacturing industries, although it is not prolific, and Lean is still very common (Reh, 2020; Socconini & Reato, 2018; Vieth & Smith, 2008). Some teams loosely use Agile methods, such as sprints, for parts of their work but not as a sole method for R&D.

Implications of Compliance Contexts for Teams

Some teams must work under rigorous compliance conditions. Consultants may find it useful to familiarize themselves with these contexts too. Compliance typically manifests as adherence to international standards, safety protocols, and privacy laws as well as compatibility with infrastructures. While compliance plays a role in engineering, government bureaucracy does not control the industry. Subspecialties and specific applications of engineering may require compliance, such as writing code for health care patient services that are governed by the Health Insurance Portability and Accountability Act (HIPAA), designing cloud storage that houses European customer data that is protected under the General Data Protection Regulation (GDPR), developing energy that is governed by the U.S. Federal Energy Regulatory Commission, and designing structures that are governed by local building and safety codes (European Union, 2018; Federal Energy Regulatory Commission, 2020; U.S. Department of Health and Human Services, 2017).

Pharmaceutical and Life Sciences Industries: Food and Drug Administration Process

Drug development teams work in complex, rapidly changing, highly regulated environments. It takes on average 10 to 15 years and researching approximately 10,000 molecules to launch a single new product to market (Pattanaik, 2014). Each drug project contains numerous moving parts involving many different organizational functions that require people of many different backgrounds meeting sometimes competing objectives to work together toward a common goal of delivering a therapy to patients.

The FDA—and equivalent government regulatory authorities in other countries—requires drug and medical device developers to follow a specific sequence of procedures that cannot be skipped or shifted around (U.S. Food & Drug Administration, 2018). In drug development, medical device development, and health care in general, human safety is paramount. Similar to software developers, research scientists and health care practitioners tend to be very specialized, but they also tend to be highly educated. It is not uncommon for life scientists to have a doctoral degree, a medical degree, or both, and many have university postdoctoral research and training experiences as well. What this means is that they have spent their formative years in the academic world, which is quite different from the corporate world. Scientific research also differs from software development and engineering because it tends to take a long time and because project goals tend to be measured in years and even decades, not months.

The FDA's Drug Development Process

The FDA drug and device development process is depicted in Figure 5.2, and a glossary of common terms is presented in Table 5.1. Drugs—such as

Discovery and Concept Development	Preclinical Research	Clinical Research	FDA Review	Post Market Safety Monitoring
• Target identification and validation • Hit discovery • Assay development and screening • Hit to lead • Lead optimization	• In vivo, in vitro testing • Proof of concept • Drug delivery • Dose range • IND application	• Phase I: Healthy volunteer study • Phases II–III: Patient population studies • Pharmacokinetics • Dose escalation • Safety • Efficacy	• NDA, ANDA, BLA application • FDA approval • Drug registration	• FDA adverse event reporting system

Figure 5.2

U.S. Food and Drug Administration (FDA) drug and device development process. IND = investigational new drug; NDA = new drug application; ANDA = abbreviated new drug application; BLA = biologics license application.

penicillin—used to be discovered accidentally (or incidentally) by applying the ingredients in existing medications to new scenarios. Now scientists can systematically reverse engineer treatments by identifying a gene or protein in the human body that plays a significant role in a disease and screening large numbers of molecular compounds to find one that will interact with it to deliver a desirable therapeutic result. Once drug candidates are identified, scientists can test them in the lab and after that in humans. This process includes structured and highly regulated steps and environments.

Ways Organizational Consultants Can Help Teams in Pharma and Life Sciences

Because it is so easy to get drawn into the expansive details of therapeutic and medical device development, organizational consultants can help scientists to become more aware of the larger picture, to be more attuned to the competitive market in anticipating changes, and to focus on how their work fits into business goals for the organization. Patient concerns, safety protocols, financial backing, and research participant recruiting strategies, for example, are all issues outside of the lab that are some of the biggest contributors to failure of clinical trials (Fogel, 2018). Organizational consultants can help leaders in life sciences set up systems to track these issues. Consultants can also help leaders in these fields improve cross-functional collaboration and team collaboration in general and can help academically trained leaders to learn to value teamwork and shared success.

Communication is a core developmental need for many scientists, not just those in life sciences. Consultants can customize their communications consulting to focus on examples that include scientists and technical leaders. The Alda Center, for example, which was started by the well-known actor Alan Alda, provides training for interdisciplinary scientific teams. This training builds on the work the Center has been doing to help scientists better communicate their research and findings to larger audiences. The Center's training is based on building empathy—helping scientists imagine how their audiences think and feel so that they can engage in communications that will build trust and land effectively with people. As Alan Alda put it,

> Effective science communication happens when we listen and connect. It happens when we use empathy. Communication is headed for success when we pay more attention to what the other person is understanding rather than focusing solely on what we want to say. (https://www.aldacenter.org/)

In fast-moving, rapidly changing organizations, effective communication systems (e.g., decision-making and information-sharing protocols, network structures, communication technology) are critically important. When autonomous teams, cross-functional projects, and matrixed leadership are the norm, miscommunication and ambiguous decisions are the result. In addition to using communication tools from the psychological literature, organizational consultants can familiarize themselves with processes, frameworks, and project management tools that are frequently employed in scientific teams (Appelo, 2016; Van den Berg & Pietersma, 2014).

Consulting to Virtual and Global Teams

Virtual and global teams are very common in tech teams. STEM and other tech companies often employ people across geographical boundaries because they are well equipped to work remotely. Offshoring is also common since talented people in other countries can often be employed. Collaborations and outsourcing are common in the pharmaceutical industry. It is typical in this industry to have one company developing a therapy and another manufacturing it. Academics collaborate across universities in a similar way. Organizational consultants can help virtual and global teams in a number of ways, including selecting team members and structuring the processes to make it work (Lauring & Jonasson, 2018).

Tech workers have been working remotely for a long time, with Cisco Systems, a prolific network communications company, leading the way back in the 1990s (Cisco Systems, n.d.). Many small tech companies are entirely virtual to save money on office expenses and to gain access to a wide range of talent. A remote job fit is also good for software development because the work does not need to be done in person. Scientists and engineers, on the other hand, often need to work in labs or on site, and these jobs are less able to be conducted virtually (Sorenson et al., 2003). Compared with other industries, organizational culture in technical industries tends to employ flatter hierarchies and more autonomous work, which is also conducive to virtual team success.

Research has found that a combination of characteristics of the job, the organization, and the person need to exist for remote work to succeed (Connell et al., 2003). A person's preferences and personality traits are important for virtual work to succeed (Brahm & Kunze, 2012; Luse et al., 2013; Ortiz de Guinea et al., 2012). As demonstrated during the COVID quarantine, when so many people were working virtually, some people thrived while others suffered (Meagher & Cheadle, 2020). Technical people may have challenges succeeding at virtual work because of their personalities. Research shows that both highly introverted and extraverted people are not well suited for exclusively virtual work (Luse et al., 2013). Extraverts may suffer from loneliness and isolation when working virtually, and introverts, though comfortable with this way of working, may fail to communicate sufficiently. Technical teams, often composed of introverted, analytical personalities, also tend to be interpersonally challenged, regardless of whether they involve in-person or virtual work. When introverted team members are remote and unseen by each other, especially if they are prone to avoiding video interactions, they can easily become even more disconnected and unaware of interpersonal problems that may be occurring.

The general challenges for technical teams and the general problems for virtual teams are no different from those for intact nontechnical teams; they are just amplified. Virtual teams may be sensitive to certain factors, such as the length of the team engagement (Ortiz de Guinea et al., 2012). For example, one team of scientists in the therapeutic industry spent the first 3 months of the COVID quarantine using e-mail and voice-only communications. They were challenged because the team was new and the members had not yet established working relationships based on trust. The team leader was highly introverted and very reluctant to use video communication. Part of the consultant's intervention for this team was to introduce video communication. Once the leader used the video technology, he was pleasantly surprised by how much more dynamic the team interaction was and how happy they all were to see each other. In another example, a team of engineers in the defense aerospace industry was using voice-only communication during the quarantine for security reasons. They fared much better because they had been working together for years and really understood each other. Their leader was also much more geared toward building relationships and constantly checked in with people to see how they were doing.

Trust, communication, culture, motivation, and performance management challenges are magnified for virtual and technical teams (Brahm & Kunze, 2012). These "people issues" can deteriorate when work is done only virtually, for example, when team members do not resolve conflicts as they arise because they are communicating asynchronously. In these areas, organizational consultants can be of particular help. In addition, virtual teams are often distributed across the globe and therefore have the added complexity of cross-cultural teamwork, leading to subtle misunderstandings that may not be worked out. Technical leaders are generally not well prepared for cross-cultural leadership and have to learn on the job (Chaudhuri & Alagaraja, 2014). Technical leaders who are transactional in nature may be unaware that some team members may feel excluded. For example, if some team members are native speakers in the language being spoken and others are not, the nonnative speakers may not feel as comfortable communicating, and the native speakers may dominate. Openness to language diversity has been shown to improve cross-cultural communication when language differences exist (Lauring & Jonasson, 2018).

Cultural values and norms also affect the effectiveness of cross-cultural teams. Technical leaders who are task oriented may not be prepared for or as tolerant of culturally different ways of doing things. Dr. Matt Barney, the vice president and director of the Infosys Leadership Institute, shared his experience of being an American learning to lead in India (Chaudhuri & Alagaraja, 2014). He said that moving to India required him to completely change the way he lived. He noted that it was critical for him to build relationships to gain access to information and commented on how important it was to observe hierarchies, to navigate corruption, and to generally be patient with things not working. How does one learn these lessons working virtually with a remote team of a different culture?

Organizational consultants have many tools to help technical leaders manage cross-cultural remote teams, such as methods of creating safety for differences; establishing mutually agreeable ground rules, norms, and expectations for collaboration; running effective virtual meetings; building relationships among team members; and managing performance. Communication tools are paramount. For example, in the case example of a U.S. company offshoring some work to the Philippines, a strong communication plan was an effective way to overcome cultural differences in values, such as punctuality and deference to authority, as well as logistical challenges, such as the time difference (Crayon et al., 2017).

Diversity and Inclusion in Technical Teams

Why does diversity (e.g., of culture, ethnicity, gender, education, expertise, socioeconomic level, personality, sexual orientation, ability status, age) matter in scientific teams? In addition to social and moral reasons, diversity is critical for excellence, access to the best talent, long-term growth, and competitiveness (Gibbs, 2014). Business and psychological studies have shown that diversity not only improves problem solving, analytical thinking, creativity, and innovation, but it also generates measurable financial return (Gompers & Kovvali, 2018). Gompers and Kovvali (2018) found that among venture capitalists, investment partners who shared the same ethnicity had an investment success rate 26% to 32% lower than investment partners of varying ethnicities.

Dr. Bernardo Ferdman (2021), an expert on diversity and inclusion, wrote that "diversity involves the differences and similarities among people across many dimensions represented in a particular group or organization" (p. 6). For example, diverse groups can benefit from differences in experience and perspective, including cultural, ethnic, gender, educational, expertise, socioeconomic, personality, sexual orientation, ability status, generational, and age differences, among others (Ferdman et al., 2021).

In team interventions, both organizational consultants and HR leaders can educate technical teams on what it means to be inclusive and can help them examine and improve their inclusivity (American Psychological Association, 2019). Ferdman (2021) stated that inclusion requires both a certain mindset and a broad skillset. One of the foundations of inclusive leadership is equity. Allocations, power, and process need to be fair and just to the members in the group. Technical fields tend to be based on meritocracy, which, in principle should be equitable, but there are deep-rooted assumptions and cultures that have been shown to be unfair (see, e.g., Gavet, 2021, and the discussion in Chapter 6, this volume). To be inclusive means to be constantly evaluating and questioning whether the group members are being treated fairly and to be reanalyzing assumptions that people may bring to the group. It means noticing and eliminating bias and discrimination within the group, and consultants can facilitate processes for teams to self-examine.

To help technical team members who might benefit from becoming more aware of the state of diversity in their industries and their organizations and from learning about business case benefits for diversity and inclusion, it can be useful for organizational consultants to provide teams with appropriate business and financial statistics from the business literature and newspapers and magazines. Other sources for data include corporate websites, reports from research organizations such as Pew Research, the Department of Labor, and Catalyst. Books and blogs that appeal to technical leaders—often written by them—also present case examples and arguments that may help convince them to take action. The key is to present data, evidence, and logical reasons to attract their attention and settle any skepticism. For example, a study by the Boston Consulting Group found that management teams with greater diversity reported an innovation revenue 19% higher than that of companies with below-average leadership diversity (Lorenzo et al., 2018). The World Economic Forum has data showing that immigration increases innovation and economic performance in cities, regions, and countries (e.g., New York, London, Singapore, the United States; Eswaran, 2019). One study suggests that immigrants to the United States generate more patentable technology than native-born Americans and are more likely to become Nobel Laureates in physics, chemistry, physiology, or medicine (Nunn et al., 2018).

The National Society of Professional Engineers is an example of a place at which technical leaders are communicating with each other. An article on their website provides reasons that engineers should care about diversity and includes data showing how diversity increases innovation and profitability, that diversity does not lower standards, and that evaluating a company's culture to make it more relevant to a diverse talent pool can increase diversity when the talent pool seems small (Why should I care about diversity in engineering, 2020). Github, *Ars Technica*, *Wired*, *Fast Company*, and *PC Magazine* are just a few of the places technical leaders go for news and book recommendations; they all have articles on diversity.

Compared with those in traditionally managed teams, autonomous teams in technical organizations may be less connected to the organization's goals and policies and more likely to generate their own ways of doing things. It may be harder to monitor their compliance, and they may resist authority coming in to keep them aligned (Angermuller, 2017; Denning, 2018). Consultants and HR leaders can stay in touch with teams to monitor their progress and offer to help them out, to offload work, such as writing job descriptions, screening candidates, conducting outreach, anything that will save them time and help them perform better.

In general, consultants and HR leaders can provide technical teams with processes and best practices to follow to help them increase diversity (American Psychological Association, 2019; Ferdman, 2021). Several examples of straightforward things to offer busy people to increase diversity and inclusion are steps to follow to broaden outreach in recruiting, specific adjustments to make to their candidate screening and search procedures to ensure a more diverse pool for hiring and promoting, mentoring programs for technical people to build close relationships with different people as well as advance their own leadership skills, and specific language that is more inclusive (Stahl, 2020; White, 2009).

SUMMARY

Technical teams, although not fundamentally different from other teams, may experience certain challenges from the makeup of their technical team members, the frameworks they employ, the structures of the organizations in which they work, and the contexts of their industries. For example, organizational consultants may encounter tensions in technical teams stemming from differences between innovative and results-oriented goals or among personalities. Technical teams often deal with complex problems that may span multiple disciplines, and the multidisciplinary makeup of the teams can cause members to have conflicting objectives, viewpoints, and approaches. Technical teams often work within a rapidly changing, matrixed organization in which leadership boundaries and decision making are overlapping or ambiguous.

Organizational consultants may find the rapid-growth leadership model in Figure 5.1 useful to work with technical teams in these contexts. Organizational consultants will also likely find that their clients employ certain methodologies or frameworks or that they work in highly regulated industries that govern how teams are structured and what their goals are. Consultants may want to familiarize themselves with appropriate frameworks, such as Agile, and regulatory standards, such as those of the FDA. Last, virtual teams are very common, and the uneven representation of women and some racial/ethnic minority groups creates other challenges for technical teams, and consulting interventions could help resolve a variety of problems.

Organizational consultants may be asked by team leaders to help teams become more efficient and high performing, or the consultants may be brought in by HR or leaders higher up in the organization, people who see how much team dysfunction is costing the organization. Consultants may find the methods described in this chapter helpful to determine the language and approaches that motivate their client teams to invest the time in focusing on the people relationships to achieve their project goals. The team frameworks and contexts described in this chapter may also be helpful to consultants working at the individual and organizational levels. The next chapter focuses on organizational-level consulting and elaborates more on the contexts in which technical teams function.

6

Consulting at the Organizational Level: Assessing and Changing Technical Organizations

So far in this book, the focus has been on the individual and team levels of technical leader consultation. In this chapter, consulting at the organizational level is considered. At the tech organizational (systemic) level, consulting often centers on big-picture issues, such as helping to formulate the vision and strategy for the organization, establishing or changing the organization's culture, hiring and retaining the right people, and identifying and helping to fix organizational-level performance problems. Consultants working at the systemic level often need to get top-level buy-in from the CEO, board, or executive levels. Technical organizations tend to be complex and rapidly changing, and technical leaders tend to be focused more on projects than on the people (e.g., Adams, 2008; Bäcklander, 2019; BlessingWhite, 2013; Felder et al., 2016; Pattanaik, 2014). Thus, consultants will likely need to demonstrate to technical leaders the value of what the consulting can offer. It is particularly important when working at the senior

https://doi.org/10.1037/0000270-007
Consulting to Technical Leaders, Teams, and Organizations: Building Leadership in STEM Environments, by J. B. Connell

levels to convey expert knowledge and value from the first contact. This chapter focuses particularly on helping organizational consultants learn how to get top-level leaders' attention, garner their trust, and provide the tools to help their organizations succeed.

The chapter begins with an overview of the people challenges that senior technical leaders face, then covers the challenges that organizational consultants face when working with them. I use the consulting process model presented in Chapter 3 to describe the kinds of consulting interventions and challenges at the organizational level in each phase of consulting. The chapter also considers several typical organizational-level topics and the ways in which they apply specifically to technical organizations. It closes with a summary of issues that are pertinent to consulting at the organizational level to technical organizations.

TOP PEOPLE-ORIENTED CHALLENGES FOR TECHNICAL ORGANIZATIONS

Figure 6.1 shows specific factors that challenge technical organizations, obtained from the interview data collected for this book (see Chapters 1 and 2). As the figure shows, the challenges tend to center on the exceptionally complex and rapidly changing nature of technical organizations.

Organizational consultants and human-resources (HR) leaders who understand how technical teams work can make a big impact in technical organizations by improving talent management processes to help attract,

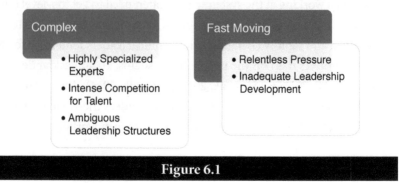

Figure 6.1

Top people challenges that technical leaders report for their organizations.

hire, and retain highly skilled technical employees. Organizational consultants and HR leaders can offer business processes and leadership structures to help with the management, communication, and decision making in technical organizations as well as assessments to determine how satisfied and engaged employees are and how well they are performing (Huber, 2011). They can also help leaders understand the benefits of diversity and recognize how increasing employee wellness and managing work–life balance can increase performance and reduce turnover (Ferdman et al., 2021).

Organizational consultants may encounter similar people-oriented challenges in small start-ups, but the consulting opportunities may differ (Berman, 2019; Greiner, 1998; Lowman, 2016). For example, large companies often have dedicated departments for HR, leadership development, and diversity/equity/inclusion, whereas small companies may not have even a single in-house HR person. This lack of HR support can leave the technical leaders fending for themselves when it comes to hiring and managing people. Large companies typically have infrastructures available to leaders for managing teams, communication, and cross-functional collaboration (Bang & Midelfart, 2017). Conversely, small companies tend to be more seat-of-the-pants, but the leaders are typically more empowered to make decisions and get things done (Lowman, 2016). Consultants working with large companies may want to get training in enterprise software management systems, such as Salesforce for customer-relationship management, Slack for instant messaging, and AWS for cloud computing. They may also want to have large-scale resources available, such as SurveyMonkey to run surveys, iCIMS to handle recruiting, or Monday to manage projects. Consultants working with start-ups may want to provide creative, low-cost solutions, and they should be prepared to educate technical leaders on the human side of work.

CHALLENGES WHEN CONSULTING TO TECHNICAL ORGANIZATIONS

When addressing systemwide issues, such as organizational assessment, culture, and performance, consultants may work with leaders at the highest level, including the CEO and other C-Suite leaders. Consultants may be surprised by some of the challenges of working with top-level technical leaders on systemwide issues. It is not unusual for consultants to feel that they have gone back in time when dealing with some technical organizations, wondering how such modern companies could be so out of touch with modern people-management methods and leadership expectations. I share two examples from my own consulting experience.

Earlier in my career, a consulting team and I were invited to present to the CEO of a large medical device company. A senior leader in learning and development (L&D) was hoping to hire us to conduct a companywide leadership assessment and then to focus on leader development and succession planning. The program was to start with the executive-level leaders. The CEO sat at the head of the table watching us file into the executive conference room and said to us, "Psychology is a bunch of bullshit." Being the most junior member of the team and the only woman in the room, I looked around for cues on how to react to his statement. Everyone nervously gave him an obligatory chuckle and sat down. I followed suit. We did the presentation, the L&D team told us it was great, but we did not get the job. The CEO did not approve the project.

A similar thing happened some years later when I walked into a smaller conference room at a start-up biotech company to present a similar type of talent management program. This time, I was the leader of the team, and I was there alone, representing the team. The CEO did not use the same language, but it was clear from his posturing and snarky comments that he was thinking the same thing. This time, however, I spoke to him eye-to-eye, commanding his respect while the VP of HR squirmed in her seat. He signed off on the program, but it did not have the intended impact because, ultimately, he had not really bought into it. Without his leadership, others did not take it seriously.

These cases illustrate an ongoing problem in technical organizations: that the HR function is not always taken seriously (Charan et al., 2011). In many technical companies, I have seen HR leaders at the highest levels lack much real authority because the technical leaders do not value what they do. *Fast Company*'s well-circulated magazine article, "Why We Hate HR" (Hammonds, 2005), described HR as often being stuck in the details of rules and efficiency and lacking the big-picture understanding of business and value. Unfortunately, HR's lack of big-picture thinking still holds true today in many organizations (KPMG, 2020).

If consultants want to attract the attention of organizational leaders and gain credibility in the C-Suite to conduct organizationwide interventions, they need to focus on adding value, not on adding rules and training courses. They need to bring solutions that demonstrably increase the company's competitive edge and add value to customers. Consultants also need to be able to stand up to the tech execs and push back when asked to do things that conflict with the consultant's professional knowledge or ethical principles. They need to put their best people forward at the organizational level—consultants who are sharp and knowledgeable; who impress very smart, demanding, often brusque technical leaders; and who are able and willing to hold them accountable.

Organizational consultants may have difficulty persuading technical CEOs to let them assess or change their organizations. In her book, *Trampled by Unicorns: Big Tech's Empathy Problem and How to Fix It,* Gavet (2021) described how the tech culture promotes a certain kind of high-level leader. She described the "Steve Jobs Syndrome" (p. 19) as the belief not only that being an extremely smart and talented individual excuses acting badly but also that a founder/CEO must be badly behaved to be a genius. Inappropriate behaviors may be accepted or excused because the individual is viewed as a misunderstood, lonely, socially awkward yet brilliant nerd. Epstein and Shelton (2019) called this phenomenon the "brilliant jerk conundrum," and, in their book of the same name, they offered some solutions. Some of their suggestions concerning problematic CEOs were directed to venture capitalists, who have a certain level of power because they control the money and they often sit on the organization's board of directors. Even so, their power may be limited, and their suggestions may center on influencing the CEO and complacent board members through developing close relationships, asking the right questions, and engaging in discussions about best practices. Epstein and Shelton also suggested bringing as much diversity as possible onto the board and the executive team as an antidote to an audacious CEO.

Organizational consultants and HR leaders can use the same tactics to gain respect and be taken seriously: building relationships with board members and the top organizational leaders, asking questions, engaging in discussions, and encouraging diversity. In fact, in the second experience I shared, the CEO of the start-up signed off on the talent management program because a particularly influential member of the board of advisors insisted he do it. Unfortunately, as the CEO of this start-up demonstrated, insisting on an intervention does not necessarily solve the problem, especially if the CEO gaslights the intervention by not taking it seriously, causing others to doubt the existence of the problem. In cases like this, the consultant may want to insist on working with the board in addition to the organizational leaders and ensure the CEO is held accountable for their participation.

THE ORGANIZATIONAL CONSULTING PROCESS IN TECHNICAL ORGANIZATIONS

The organizational consulting process depicted in Figures 3.1 and 3.2 also applies when working at the organizational level. The model includes four phases: (a) getting the technical leader's attention, (b) delivering assessment feedback to the organizational leader, (c) implementing organizational change, and (d) evaluating the success of the change. When consulting at the organizational level, the model refers to working with top-level leaders, typically in the C-Suite, and assessing, changing, and evaluating organizationwide interventions. The following sections describe challenges that organizational consultants may face when consulting at the organizational level to technical leaders.

Getting the Technical Leader's Attention

Even with dealing with nonabrasive technical leaders, it may hard for a consultant to get the attention of high-level leaders, especially when their energies are already tapped out by having to lead in a rapidly changing complex environment. What's more, highly specialized experts are likely to be highly focused on specific issues. That focus is what enabled them to become experts. When organizational consultants and HR leaders want to bring technical experts' attention to people problems, they may find that technical leaders are unaware of their existence or not appreciative of the importance of these problems. For example, when cash is running low and a technical leader is worried about the next round of funding, a CEO or senior leader is not likely to be interested in hearing how to keep their employees satisfied. Even when their companies are not in crisis mode, tech leaders might simply prefer to focus on the technology, often their preferred comfort zone. The CEO of the large medical device company discussed earlier, for example, was very confident in the company's technology but was unaware that they did not have a leadership succession plan and did not know what the consequences would be if a key leader left unexpectedly.

The attract–support–explain model (see Figure 3.3) suggests ways to get senior technical leaders' attention. This model can be used to focus on top leaders' perceived needs for the organization. Similarly, consultants can tie the people issues to enhancing employees' ability to meet their technical goals. Making a case to a technical leader might sound like this:

> Would you agree that a major way you'll beat the competitor to market is if you keep the best people working on this product? If they leave because they are frustrated, exhausted, or burned out, you will incur downtime while you find replacements and get them up to speed.

Even though it seems counterproductive to encourage employees to take vacation days, a positive vacation culture can help employees feel happier and be more productive at work. For example, one study found that over 75% of managers agreed that vacation improves employees' focus and alleviates burnout (Frye, 2018).

Collecting Data and Delivering Organizational Diagnostic Feedback to Senior Technical Leaders

When delivering feedback and making recommendations at the organizational level, organizational consultants and HR leaders are often focused on the employee-related issues in the organization, such as turnover, productivity, and diversity. By contrast, technical leaders who are low in

empathy may not see what matters to employees. I call this lack of awareness the *disconnect challenge*, as shown in Figure 3.2. For example, the
turnover for women at a company may be high, and the leader may think
the company is offering all employees good compensation and benefits—
everything that looks good on paper—but not understand why the women
say it is also important for them to have friendships and fun at work.
Citing the research might help validate the findings. For example, in a
Gallup global employee engagement survey (Mann, 2018), women who
strongly agreed they had a best friend at work were more than twice as
likely to be engaged than women who said otherwise (63% vs. 29%).

Entitlement and deeply engrained defensiveness may also surface as
resistance. The example of the growing biotech company was classic—the
technical teams all had excessively positive ratings of themselves and others.
By contrast, Scripps Healthcare responded very positively to authentic
feedback they received on their inquiry into why they had a high rate of
turnover, especially among first-year employees (Cahill & Sedrak, 2012).
One of the major differences between these two examples is that Scripps
was experiencing a significant financial setback, and the high turnover
rate was costing them a lot of money. High-level leaders were thus eager to
make change. The intervention was initially to conduct an organizationwide
survey as well as targeted interviews and focus groups to understand the
root causes of the high turnover. The results indicated that employees of
different generations had very different ways of evaluating the workplace,
measuring their own satisfaction, and deciding whether to stay or go. The
organization had previously used a one-size-fits-all approach to communicate with employees and offer them benefits, but by doing so, they missed
the different needs of people with different generational communication
styles and the benefits people needed at different phases of life. The ensuing
change effort focused on revising organizational communication and benefits to appeal better to diverse groups of employees.

Consulting on Implementing Organizationwide Change

Although rapid change is core to technical industries, changing a technical organization as a whole can be challenging. Technical organizations

commonly have ambiguous leadership, autonomous teams, and flatter hierarchies, and this combination makes holistic organizational change more difficult than it would be in an organization with clear top-down leadership (BlessingWhite, 2013; Hogg et al., 2012; Kleinman, 2017; Pandya, 2014). Organizational consultants and HR leaders may need to help the leadership work through the ways in which a systematic change would take place. This process would include consideration of ways to obtain employee buy-in. If the prototypical scientist personality traits of skepticism and autonomy run high in an organization, it may prove challenging to persuade people to change their behavior (Chen & Simpson, 2015; Rasoal et al., 2012; Rounds et al., 2021; Sato, 2016).

Andy Deakins was the director of human resources and safety at Young Touchstone, a manufacturing organization located in Tennessee. Crane's (2018) book, *The Rise of the Coachable Leader*, discusses how Deakins described one highly successful example of changing the management culture of the organization from command-and-control to a collaborative, coaching culture (pp. 88–93). The challenge was to integrate two rival manufacturing organizations that had merged and to shift their bitter competitiveness to collaboration across the organization. The intervention was to hire Tom Crane, an organizational consultant, to partner with the director of HR to introduce his "The Heart of Coaching" toolkit to all managers, from the president to front-line supervisors, simultaneously in a training workshop. Although some individual managers initially resisted the process, as the entire organization changed over time through continued interventions and accountability checks, many came to see the value of the new way of managing, especially engineering and quality managers who moved from being bosses to being coaches and found they had their pick of the best employees.

It can be helpful for consultants to work within the technical team frameworks to increase buy-in and customize to individual team dynamics in autonomous teams and specific contexts of the organization, such as how quickly products need to be released to customers. Agile, Lean Six Sigma, and the FDA development process are all examples of frameworks that are typically used by technical organizations. Consultants may suggest, for instance, adding a piece into all Agile retro meetings (see Chapter 5) to address how the team could have been more inclusive during the sprint as a way to shift the organizational culture to be more inclusive. Alternatively, consultants may suggest tailoring sprint lengths and interteam coordination frequency to the organizational context as a part of an organizational change effort to help teams collaborate more effectively with each other (Gustavsson, 2019). These types of change interventions are not atypical for organizational consultants; they are just customized to the technical environments, using the language the organizations use.

Evaluating the Success of Organizational Change Efforts

It may be hard for consultants to conduct formal evaluations of consulting projects in organizations because clients may not want to spend the time or money. Fast-moving, rapidly changing technical organizations are no exception. One of the challenges to conducting an evaluation is that senior leaders may change positions. They may not stay in place long enough after a project is complete to determine the effects of an intervention. If the results of an evaluation are negative, their judgment to have undertaken it may be questioned. When organizations do undertake evaluations of change efforts, they may have difficulty agreeing on the outcome metrics to assess. The most desirable measures tend to be financial, but the work of consultants is often not directly tied to financial results. Helping technical leaders appreciate success in indirect ways is part of the consultant's and the HR leader's challenge.

It is also important not to overstep and lose credibility by trying to claim financial gains without sufficient data to support them. For example, many costs of turnover are not direct, such as the impact to morale on others and the lowered productivity of employees who were disengaged before leaving (Salicru, 2020). Turnover can be translated into monetary costs, but it may be more meaningful to describe the amount of time managers lose by having to step in to do the work of the employee, searching for and interviewing new candidates, and training a new hire, as exemplified in the case examples of Young Touchstone and Scripps Healthcare.

For example, within 5 years of the initial inquiry at Scripps Healthcare, revenues had increased by $130 million, turnover had decreased by 8.5% for first-year employees, and the organization had received awards from *Working Mother Magazine* and AARP for being a great place to work (Cahill & Sedrak, 2012).

For technical leaders who crave data, it can be easier to get buy-in for evaluation at the beginning of an organizational intervention. When outcome evaluations are integrated into the project and the initial and final assessments are tied together with clear metrics for evaluating any improvement associated with the interventions, technical leaders have tangible ways to make decisions on whether it is worth the investment. Scientists have an added reason to conduct evaluations of organizational effectiveness—their funders require it. The National Science Foundation (NSF) recently added a requirement that project evaluation be part of all grant proposals (Frechtling, 2010). Project evaluations are not just evaluations of the science; they are evaluations of how well the project is run, and some of that falls into the realms of organizational consulting and HR. There are evaluators who specialize in NSF-funded research as well as other grant-funded research who may be good partners for consultants who work with nationally funded organizations. The American Evaluation Association and Better Evaluation are places to learn more (see https://www.eval.org/ and https://www.betterevaluation.org/en).

COMMON TOPICS OF SYSTEMWIDE INTERVENTIONS IN TECHNICAL ORGANIZATIONS

Organization-level consulting typically addresses such things as assessing and changing the process, structure, and culture of the organization, mostly centering on people issues, such as employee satisfaction, engagement, performance, hiring, equity, and turnover (Lowman, 2016). Naturally, technical organizations also have to deal with all of these, but a few key areas come up a lot, as described in Chapters 1 and 2. These areas are talent management, communication, organizational values and culture, and diversity/equity/inclusion. These topics are addressed in the following sections.

Talent Management

Attracting and retaining technical talent throughout the organization is one of the biggest challenges for many technical organizations (Cappelli, 2019). The legendary tech organizations (e.g., Google, NASA, Johnson & Johnson) are very famous, pay well, and usually have little trouble attracting talent. Others, less well known, may attract talent by their missions, helping to solve exciting problems like curing cancer, developing artificial intelligence, or transporting humans to Mars. Other technical organizations, however, typically have to work harder to attract and retain technical people. They may have to compete for talent in different ways. But those attractors are not just financial.

BlessingWhite (2013) found that technical employees generally have six workplace needs to feel satisfied and engaged: (a) achievement, (b) autonomy, (c) professional identification, (d) participation in mission and goals, (e) collegial support and sharing, and (f) keeping current. These are organizational factors with which consultants can help. There are other enticing factors too, such as being a start-up, which attracts technical people who enjoy the thrill of building a company or who envision an opportunity to make a large amount of money. Exemplary diversity and inclusion opportunities are important for some technical leaders. Other potential attractors include financial stability and the opportunity to work from home.

Organizational consultants and HR leaders can help tech companies make jobs more appealing and emphasize different factors in recruiting and promoting to attract and retain technical talent. Technical leaders, however, often take on both hiring and promoting technical people into leadership positions, as described in Chapter 2, and may not want help from HR. When they make hiring decisions, they tend to put the technical skills requirement first. This can weed out good potential leaders who have good interpersonal skills and good, but not exemplary, technical skills or who have good technical skills but are intimidated by the process (Behroozi et al., 2020). They may also, perhaps unwittingly, hire people whom they see as being like themselves, which can increase or maintain homogeneity in teams (Behroozi et al., 2020; Cappelli, 2019). Organizational consultants and HR professionals have an opportunity to show that they can improve the outcome by getting involved. They need to show that they can select people who are able to lead technical teams better and who will stick around longer and be liked and respected by others more than the people the technical leaders would have hired on their own. They can also show how putting together standard hiring processes and training technical people who are involved in interviewing can reduce bias.

A chief HR officer who had worked in several medium-sized life sciences companies described a common challenge rapidly growing companies face in identifying and promoting technical leaders: "In a small, high-growth company, many times individuals are promoted quickly . . . because they are in place, not necessarily because they're demonstrating leadership aptitude" (personal communication by an individual who did not wish to be cited by name, April 3, 2020). Some large companies have leadership pipelines and plan out growth from an organizational perspective, but as described in Chapter 1, succession planning is easily overlooked in rapidly changing, complex organizations of any size if leaders are stretched thin, overworked, and focused on meeting project goals. Putting together leadership pipelines and succession planning processes are areas in which organizational consultants can help with talent management.

Unlike in the medical device company described earlier, some technical leaders recognize the value of a data-driven approach to succession planning. For example, one pharmaceutical company hired our team to assess their entire leadership team of more than 50 directors, vice presidents, and C-Suite officers and to help them form a succession management plan. The president of the company said it was the first time they had made promotions based on data, rather than on who liked the candidate. Not surprisingly, the company was not very diverse, and the performance data helped the people in the outgroup to be promoted.

Companies have also brought data-driven approaches to talent management using people analytics, in which large amounts of data are collected through computer usage and the data are analyzed to determine workplace performance trends (Leonardi & Contractor, 2018). For example, as described in Chapter 4, Google developed their leadership framework using data analytics to statistically determine the managerial behaviors that correlated with high satisfaction ratings from their employees. Microsoft created what turned out to be a very controversial "productivity score," devised from data they collected from employees at organizations who used the Microsoft Teams collaboration platform to communicate with each other (O'Flaherty, 2020). Once employees and privacy advocates learned how much users were being tracked and what kinds of judgments were being made about their microlevel behaviors, they began raising concerns. Data privacy has become an international concern, and many governments have set up regulations, such as HIPAA and GDPR, to protect people (European Union, 2018; U.S. Department of Health and Human Services, 2017).

Organizationwide and Systems Communication

Communication was one of the top challenges for technical leaders, as reported in Chapter 2. The organization's infrastructure plays a key role in facilitating communication across functions, across levels, and externally, especially in rapidly changing industries. For example, bureaucracy, politics, misalignment, distributed teams, and siloed management are some aspects of the infrastructure that can potentially slow and distort communication and trust across the organization (Covey, 2006; Martin et al., 2015). Shifting priorities is a common challenge for tech companies, and senior leaders may need help conveying new priorities to the appropriate levels of the organization (Fournier, 2017). Consultants can help technical organizations improve communication systems and processes and shift organizational cultures and values to be more collaborative, customer oriented, and feedback driven; such changes will improve both internal and external communication. The health care industry, for example, has had to modify external communication systems to be more collaborative so that they can match increasing patient demands, manage acquisitions of pharmaceutical suppliers, and handle payments from insurance providers (Loria, 2019).

Because of increasing market pressures, several of the big pharma companies conducted major organizational restructuring to improve poor communication, inefficient decision making, and divisive politics (Gautam & Pan, 2016; Kleinman, 2017). They have taken lessons from smaller, more streamlined biotech companies and moved from having leaders manage large, 50- to 100-person teams in hierarchical siloed management structures to smaller, more empowered, cross-functional teams with matrixed management and more direct accountability (Kleinman, 2017). The Alda Center for Communicating Science, for example, has expanded from teaching scientists how to communicate to also helping them build effective communication infrastructures in their organizations. Laura Lindenfeld, executive director of the Alda Center, emphasized how important the organizational infrastructure was to have effective communication:

> I'd like to see more effort focused on communication systems within organizational structures. For example, when scientists are applying for grants, they're not thinking about processes and structures or a shared vision and mission, especially when it comes to management sections. . . . Considering that many scientific research papers that are coming out now are multidisciplinary, it's increasingly important to help teams develop a common language to advance their collaborative efforts. The entire process requires strong communication, whether it be writing the paper and getting it published, and then monetizing and building products. (L. Lindenfeld, personal communication, October 15, 2020)

Communication is a challenge in the software industry, as well, especially with the speed of change in that industry and the autonomy that Agile teams employ, as described in Chapter 5.

Organizational Values and Culture

Another area in which consultants and HR leaders can have an impact at the organizational level is the development of interventions that help technical organizations identify their de facto and explicit values and culture and make any needed changes. For example, when Satya Nadella took on the role of CEO at Microsoft, he hired a former McKinsey consultant to be the chief people officer (Nadella et al., 2017). In response to employee feedback, the consultant created a renewal plan for the company that, in part, consisted of shifting the culture from "know-it-alls" to "learn-it-alls." In other words, the company shifted from a culture in which people sought to prove they were the smartest person in the room—a common behavior among technical people—to a culture in which they were curious about the customer, they actively sought diversity and inclusion, and they acted in unity. Microsoft then implemented several programs to foster these new cultural values, including creating annual "hackathon" events and summits of engineers to bring together different people to share ideas and generate new and diverse products and linking executive compensation to diversity progress (Nadella et al., 2017).

Societal shifts, changing laws, and major events, such as the #MeToo and Black Lives Matter movements and the January 2020 invasion of the U.S. Capitol, have caused companies to take public positions to reassure customers, to implement training and accountability practices to meet legal requirements, and to shift their cultures to attract and retain quality talent. Because technical companies make up a large percentage of the highest revenue companies in the world, as described in Chapter 1, a lot of media attention is given to them. Organizational consultants and HR leaders have many opportunities to help create large-scale change by helping technical companies change their organizational cultures with interventions directed at aligning values, measuring attitudes, and holding employees accountable for congruent behavior.

DIVERSITY/EQUITY/INCLUSION CHALLENGES AT THE ORGANIZATIONAL LEVEL

In the interview study conducted for this book, technical leaders provided mixed descriptions of how diversity was fostered and managed in their organizations. Some leaders said their organizations were very mindful of diversity in both their hiring and their management practices, while others said it was important but not on their radar. One leader at a medium-sized company gave the example of being mindful of parents during the 2020 pandemic work-from-home mandate. When asked whether diversity was a concern at his company, a chief technology officer of a medium-sized tech company said,

> There's definitely a concern. We give overviews of our positions that are not gender- or racially biased to not deter candidates. Internally, we facilitate groups like a women's circle. There are not too many women in engineering. A few are in [quality assurance]. Harassment training enables a certain level of conversation. The whole organization is 50/50 in terms of gender parity. . . . In smaller organizations, the focus is on survival. You always want to do it better if there is a choice. Unfortunately, there is not enough energy to hire consultants and make those choices. (Personal communication by an individual who did not wish to be cited by name, April 27, 2020)

Like the technical leaders, the organizational consultants and HR leaders who were interviewed had mixed experiences with diversity in technical organizations. Some found the technical organizations they worked with to be quite diverse racially and culturally. They frequently mentioned the lack of women in the field, however, and had observations similar to those of the female technical leaders—that it was hard for women to be heard and respected, especially in global environments. The consultants also reported that some technical leaders were more aware of or focused on efforts to increase diversity than were others. In some organizations, it was a top priority; for others, it was not on their radar, not because they did not seem to care but because they were focused on other things, such as product development and sales goals.

Consulting at the Organizational Level on Diversity/Equity/Inclusion

Diversity, equity, and inclusion are concerns that ultimately need to be dealt with at the organizational level. Organizational consultants and HR leaders can help organizational leaders understand why an organization lacks diversity, the inequities that exist, and the reasons that people feel excluded, and they can lead the effort to change the situation. There are many organizational approaches to assess current levels of diversity, equity, and inclusion and to create an inclusive culture, attract diverse people, and retain them (American Psychological Association, 2019; Ferdman, 2021). Some common sticking points that consultants may run into when dealing with technical leaders include that they do not think there is a problem, they think they have done all they can and there just are not enough qualified diverse candidates, and they are afraid of doing the wrong thing and getting criticized for it. Organizational leaders may quote statistics for their organization that show large numbers of diverse employees, but the shared numbers are not necessarily of the people in STEM (science, technology, engineering, and mathematics) jobs or in leadership positions. See Chapter 4 for examples of those statistics.

In rapidly growing organizations, consultants may find that busy, overworked people are less likely to spend time reading policies and updates and are more likely to want to take shortcuts. For example, when hiring, it is much quicker and easier for technical leaders to reach out to people they know than to people they do not know to find viable candidates. Consultants and HR can help with outreach, either with specific team support or larger outreach programs to make sure the company has a presence in different organizations and universities.

Another consideration for consultants is that the lack of diversity in technical organizations often goes beyond the organization. As described in Chapter 5, diversity varies across industries in STEM. To increase diversity, equity, and inclusion within an organization, it is important to understand the larger issues in the STEM industry and in certain industries within STEM. Take, for example, women in STEM. There are far fewer women in engineering and computer science than in health care, for example, and there are far fewer women in health care leadership positions than in health care in general (Funk & Parker, 2018; Kaiser Family Foundation, 2020). It is worth exploring why. For example, a common resistance could be that there aren't enough women in this field, so we cannot hire them. The consultant could turn this statement around and help the organization offer tools or programs to attract young people of diverse backgrounds to STEM, develop diversity internships, or develop partner relationships with high schools and colleges with large numbers of underrepresented groups in STEM (Lamb et al., 2018). Then, when the time comes to hire people, those individuals who participated in the program might prioritize the company that had gotten them started.

How Do Organizational Cultures Impact Women in STEM?

Why are there so few women in engineering and tech? Why are there fewer women in high-level positions in health care? Why are some STEM fields more gender balanced than others? Masculine cultures, insufficient early experience, and gender gaps in self-efficacy are three factors that contribute to the lower numbers of women in computer science, engineering, and physics than in biology, chemistry, and mathematics (Cheryan et al., 2017). Whether intended or not, a large proportion of men in a field can reinforce a "masculine culture" that keeps women from feeling like they belong. There is also evidence to suggest that gender bias is systemic and that the meritocracy method for promoting STEM professionals does not apply equally to women and men (Castilla & Benard, 2010; Coe et al., 2019). For example, the Salk Institute in La Jolla, California, settled a high-profile gender discrimination lawsuit in 2018 in which three tenured female scientists claimed that an "old boys' club" created a hostile work environment for women that limited their advancement and kept them in smaller labs, even though they brought in more research grants (Hiltzik, 2018; Schwab, 2018).

In a survey conducted by the Pew Research Center, women in STEM jobs were more likely to report having experienced gender discrimination than women in non-STEM jobs (Funk & Parker, 2018). The frequencies were greater in STEM settings in which men outnumbered women and settings in which the women held postgraduate degrees; reports of experiencing gender discrimination were also high from people in computer jobs both inside and outside of STEM industries. Silicon Valley, where women make up less than 20% of the tech workforce, is notorious for gender bias and sexual harassment (Mundy, 2017). Some top tech companies have tried various ways to raise the percentage of women in tech and to reduce negative behaviors toward women with training on diversity and inclusion, unconscious bias, and gender-neutral hiring practices (Mundy, 2017). The results were encouraging, and consultants and HR leaders can continue to offer expertise and support to technical organizations for efforts to change their cultures to reduce bias and discrimination.

What else can organizational consultants do to help leaders in technical industries attract more women? Organizational consultants and HR leaders can play significant roles in shifting the thinking and behaviors toward women in the STEM workplace by raising awareness of the challenges women face through surveys and training, bringing more women scientists into the organization by involving leaders of all genders in outreach programs, and accelerating equity within organizations by ensuring fairness in compensation and promotions. For example, consultants could help companies become familiar with relevant research findings, including the finding that female role models and mentors are consistently cited as important factors contributing to women's success in STEM environments (Austin, 2016; Bhatia & Amati, 2010; Daly, 2014; Turner-Moffatt, 2019). In the interview study described in Chapter 2, the most common suggestion for increasing the number of women in STEM from interview participants was to reach out to girls in school when they are still young, even as young as elementary school. Male and female technical leaders who are looking to make a difference for women or who are simply looking for ways to improve their leadership skills might benefit from leading efforts to mentor girls and young women and other underrepresented groups, such as some racial and ethnic groups, LGBTQ+ people, people with disabilities, and people of different age ranges. In addition to providing guidance for mentoring and outreach programs, organizational consultants and HR leaders can help technical organizations set goals and measure progress for improving diversity, equity, and inclusion, providing the technical leaders with the data they tend to like.

On a personal note, my daughter entered college recently to study a science major. I fully supported her, but at the same time I worried that she would feel as isolated as I did as an engineer, especially because the percentage of women in STEM is still so low. During her first week of school, however, she told me she had been invited to join a sorority for women in STEM. I was initially shocked that my "nerdy" protégé would consider joining a sorority, but then I realized how desirable it would be to have "sisters" in science to support her for life. (I also wondered if my life trajectory would have been different if there had been something like that when I was in college.)

SUMMARY

Consultants working at the organizational level participate in a number of activities, including working with high-level executives or boards whose actions affect the entire organization on structural and communication issues, strategy, performance evaluation, talent management, and so on. The barriers to access in consulting to technical leaders can be high for nontechnical people. Suggestions were provided for establishing credibility with top-level technical leaders. One of the consultant's tasks is to help technical leaders appreciate the value of conducting organizational-level interventions that focus on areas such as the organizational vision, culture, talent, and infrastructure. Consultants can also be helpful in supporting senior leaders to get buy-in for change projects. Because technical organizations tend to be highly competitive, internally complex, and rapidly changing, high-level leaders are often seeking ways to increase efficiency and performance, attract and retain high quality and diverse talent, and quickly meet customer needs. Organizational consultants can use the methods outlined in this chapter, such as the attract–support–explain model, to position their efforts to offer solutions to those challenges.

7

Summary and a Look
at the Future of Consulting

Throughout this book, I have suggested that technical leaders need to branch out from the technology focus and be more business savvy and people oriented in order to be successful organizational leaders. In Chapter 1, I described how technology is rapidly moving to the forefront of business strategy for organizations across industries, not only in tech. Information technology (IT), for example, has moved from a cost center to a value center for many organizations, as products and services are now frequently being delivered by the internet and organizational infrastructures have become more technology based. IT leadership is moving from manager- and director-level positions to the C-Suite as technological leadership becomes more important to the success of organizations. Chief technology officers are becoming much more common, even in smaller companies. Chief medical officers, chief science officers, and other such

https://doi.org/10.1037/0000270-008
Consulting to Technical Leaders, Teams, and Organizations: Building Leadership in STEM Environments,
by J. B. Connell

technical positions have also become a part of the C-Suite in some industries. As such, it is important for technical leaders to learn the business to be able to contribute at a higher level and all the way up to the highest level.

I also addressed, in Chapter 1, the challenges technical leaders face because they often lack business savvy and are less skilled in people management than leaders in other industries (Balser, 2019; Chen & Simpson, 2015; Hurd, 2009; Kumar & Hsiao, 2007; Loria, 2019; Stoller et al., 2016). Throughout the book, I provided examples from interviews with technical leaders showing that they rarely prioritize training in interpersonal skills. Rather, they tend to be so focused on meeting project goals and simultaneously pressured to meet these goals that leadership training gets shelved. Technical leaders said in their own words in Chapter 2 that they needed to develop communication skills, emotional intelligence, and performance management techniques, but they often failed to make time to do it, and their leaders did not give them time even if they wanted to do it. Moreover, most scientists love being scientists: They are good at science, and that is where they are comfortable (Hurd, 2009). It makes sense for them to stay oriented in that area. One challenge for organizational consultants is to help scientists, and technical leaders in general, become more comfortable with leadership.

In addition to helping technical leaders feel more comfortable about the people and business aspects of leadership, organizational consultants can train and coach individual technical leaders on certain skills and abilities, such as managing employee performance, communicating across teams, and perceiving and managing emotions. More generally, to succeed with technical leaders as well as with technical teams and organizations, consultants may find it useful to employ the consulting model presented in Chapter 3 to appeal to technical leaders, to be conscious of the scientific mindset, and to understand the context of the technical workplace.

The model works at all three levels of consulting—individual, group, and organizational. As described in Chapter 4, two common challenges that organizational consultants often run into when consulting to individual technical leaders occur when the latter put up barriers to dealing with emotions and either are not in touch with feelings or do not see them as a valuable source of information. Table 3.1 and Chapter 4 contained recommendations for dealing with those situations to help technical leaders become more self-aware and develop empathy for others. Several technical leadership competency models were also presented to guide consultants in targeting individual development efforts with technical leaders.

Consulting at the team level can quickly become complex in technical organizations. The multidisciplinary nature of technical teams can be a source of conflict because team members have differing values, goals, and perspectives. They are also often working at a rapid pace with constant change. It can be challenging for organizational consultants to take a team "offline" long enough to help them resolve their interpersonal issues. Chapter 5 offered techniques to consult in this environment and tools that technical teams may employ to improve their productivity and cross-functional communication.

Rapid change and complexity are themes at the organizational level as well. Because technical organizations often have many moving parts and autonomous work teams, organizational consultants may find it challenging to align leadership and to conduct organizationwide interventions that are taken seriously across the organization. Chapter 6 contained suggestions for getting buy-in from top-level leadership in technical organizations to drive organizational interventions, such as changing the culture, increasing diversity, and rolling out communication and talent-management systems.

Rapidly changing environments can create a paradox. On the one hand, to stay relevant and to earn credibility among technical leaders, organizational consultants need to be continuous learners not only in the fields of consulting and human resources (HR) but also in business and technology. Consultants have to remain flexible to adapt to the constantly occurring rapid changes in technical industries as well as changes that affect organizational consulting. On the other hand, it might be wise for consultants not to get too caught up in trends because they change so quickly and require so much rework. It might be sensible to stick with proven methods of consulting and navigating change, at least to an extent. After all, people are still people. Gilmore Crosby (2021) wrote about this topic in his book, *Planned Change: Why Kurt Lewin's Social Science is Still Best Practice for Business Results, Change Management, and Human*

Progress. Consultants may need to experiment to find the right balance between these two approaches.

THE EFFECTS OF DATA AND PEOPLE ANALYTICS ON THE FUTURE OF CONSULTING

People analytics is a relatively new HR field in which professionals statistically analyze employee data to manage talent (Cappelli, 2019; DDI et al., 2018; Ihsan & Furnham, 2018; Leonardi & Contractor, 2018). Many companies, especially large ones like Google and Microsoft, have started to make use of the vast amounts of data they have collected about their employees to develop hiring and performance management systems. For example, as described in Chapter 4, Google created its 8 key management behaviors leadership model using people analytics.

The emergence of the field of people analytics raises several implications for the future of organizational consultants. First, organizational consultants have opportunities to work in people analytics. Consultants who want to work in this field will likely have to learn how to conduct and interpret complex statistical analyses using data-analysis tools (Cappelli, 2019; DDI et al., 2018; Zielinski, 2019). Examples of tools include R, Python, Excel, and Power BI, but there are many emerging data-analytics tools, and the field is rapidly changing. Consultants will likely need to become adept at researching, learning, and using new technologies. Second, there will likely be opportunities to design people-analytics tools and to work closely with technologists who develop the tools. Third, technical leaders generally love data, and they will likely expect organizational consultants to use and/or understand people-analytics tools to provide them with evidence to support future interventions. Fourth, people analytics could possibly replace a lot of the traditional assessment and development work of consultants as it becomes automated and directly accessible to organizational leaders and employees.

On the other hand, quantitative data are limited in the level of understanding of human behavior they can provide. For example, people analytics tend to focus on the attributes of employees, not the nuances of relationships between people, although the emerging field of relational analytics may address some of those factors (Leonardi & Contractor, 2018). Likely, organizational consultants will still be needed to help technical as well as nontechnical leaders understand people issues when the analytics do not provide sufficient answers.

In addition, as described in Chapter 3, technical leaders, who tend to be scientists at heart, may be inclined to focus too much on the data, and they may use the data as a form of resistance to feedback. Technical leaders who are introverted may also use technology as a shield to avoid interacting with people. Even though technical leaders may be more comfortable using data analytics to manage people issues, they might benefit more from working with people—for example, organizational consultants—to develop their people skills. After all, consultants and coaches are experts at helping leaders to explore their vulnerabilities, fears, and frustrations and to engage in high-level conversations about personalized business and leadership strategies. In the future, organizational consultants may want to differentiate themselves from technological approaches to leadership development by their interpersonal skills and expertise.

ETHICAL CONSIDERATIONS OF NEW TECHNOLOGY IN FUTURE CONSULTING

Consulting to technical organizations can be exciting because many of them create and offer impressive products and services, such as cures for terrible diseases, platforms for changing the way business is done, and new ways to entertain people. However, new technologies often raise new ethical questions. Is it okay that people become addicted to social media or drugs? Where do we draw the line when experimenting on people to develop new medical procedures, medicines, artificial intelligence, and computing technologies? How much information is okay to collect and share? How much responsibility do organizations have to protect people from vulnerabilities in technologies, such as power grids going down, autopiloted vehicles crashing, robotic surgery killing patients, automated stock trading resulting in the loss of life savings, and so on? What kinds of technologies are okay to create? Many more ethical questions need to be considered in a variety of technological domains. Organizational consultants may want to collaborate with experts in the field of business ethics to answer these sorts of questions.

There are also concerns about the way employees are treated in organizations, and these concerns are changing as new technologies are added to the workplace. Organizational consultants have opportunities to help with concerns about the effects of technology in the workplace, such as social isolation, overwork, burnout, conflict escalation, lost productivity, damaged reputations, impersonal work environments, misunderstandings, and reductions in employee and customer loyalty. Organizational consultants may find themselves delving into or partnering with people in the fields of human factors and engineering psychology to develop solutions to these problems.

NEW REALITIES FOR FUTURE CONSULTING

Virtual and distributed teams will likely continue to be increasingly common, and perhaps the norm, as communication technology improves and the world shrinks. Organizational consultants have a lot of opportunity to shape how virtual teams interact and how consultants interact with them. I offered several suggestions in Chapter 5, but many questions remain for organizational consultants to research. What are the best ways to coach online? Are there tools that can increase the coach's effectiveness rather than simply trying to simulate a face-to-face interaction? What are the best practices for running team-building interventions for remote teams? It used to be, "Get the team together!" What tools will emerge—or what tools can psychologists create—to improve team-building experiences and results? How will organizations change as they are held together only electronically? How will their human-resource needs change?

What other realities are on the horizon? Mixed-reality tools that provide video, instant messaging, and shared documents are already widely used (e.g., Zoom, Slack, Microsoft Teams), but they are just early renditions of mixed-reality tools (Murray, 2020). Artificial intelligence is only in its infancy as well, with bots (i.e., automated software programs that can be thought of as software robots) responding to HR inquiries, sending out reminders to organizational leaders to check in with their teams, and identifying and reaching out to potential new customers, patients, and hires (DDI et al., 2018; Ihsan & Furnham, 2018; Reh, 2020; Zielinski, 2019). Always-on video feeds are starting to keep remote team members connected and feeling less isolated. Drones are starting to deliver items in real time. The mixed realities of today's office workers are only glimpses into the future realities of work.

As I was writing the final pages of this book, I happened to have a conversation with Alex Howland, who worked on my assessment team as an intern while he was in graduate school studying to become an organizational consultant. He is now the CEO of a very successful completely virtual company. As a graduate student, he envisioned a virtual world in which people in organizations could conduct business as avatars (i.e., graphical pictures that represent their characters). He employed a team of software developers to create a virtual world called Virbela (https://www.virbela.com/), where people learn, develop, and conduct business using avatars. It is more than just a learning and development platform; it is a world in which organizations, including Virbela, are actually headquartered. The world in some ways reflects reality, but it is also different and better in certain ways. For example, an avatar can jump to a different place on campus instead of walking there. A global team can enjoy happy hour watching fireworks on the beach together without having to leave their desks.

Dr. Howland and his team invited me to consult with them on their effort to create an experience in Virbela to help participants metaphorically understand what happens when they embark on a project without a plan, clear communication, or shared information. It was a fun and exciting project. I had the chance to work on a multidisciplinary team with organizational consultants, software developers, and a professor who specialized in art and imagination. To build what we later named the Invisible Path game, we started with the concept of a real-life team-building exercise in which team members guide a blindfolded person through a task. We expanded on it for the virtual world where anything is possible, where employees can take risks and not get hurt, where information can appear in the air, and where consultants can offer new and exciting interactions for their clients.

The resulting game had a playful office feel that included imaginative surprises and achieved the goal of giving players an experience they could relate back to their teams at work. Technical leaders who have played the game have invariably come back energized with a deeper understanding of what they needed to do to improve teamwork on their teams. From a consulting perspective, it was a lot of fun both to design the game and to work with consultants in the virtual world. Gamification (i.e., incentivizing engagement in nongame activities using game-style mechanisms) has become popular in other domains in which organizational consultants work, such as recruiting, assessment, training, and education, and it is effectively used to attract diverse populations into the STEM workforce (Cappelli, 2019; Ihsan & Furnham, 2018; Lamb et al., 2018). When it comes to virtual consulting, future opportunities are limitless.

CONCLUSION

Organizational consultants will need to become increasingly technology savvy and business savvy, as well as data driven, to keep up with technical leaders of the future. Enormous potential exists for organizational consultants to collaborate with technical leaders on their people, business, and technology strategies. There is much that consultants can do to change lives and give people opportunities that they may never have considered or that they may not have had support to pursue. Organizational consultants, researchers, educators, and HR leaders are engineers too, and they have the power to reengineer the workplace.

References

Adams, J. U. (2008, March 7). *Drug discovery and development: A complex team sport*. AAAS. https://www.sciencemag.org/features/2008/03/drug-discovery-and-development-complex-team-sport#

Adkins, L. (2010). *Coaching Agile teams: A companion for ScrumMasters, Agile coaches, and project managers in transition*. Addison-Wesley Professional.

American Medical Association. (2014, April 24). *How med schools are preparing students for team-based care*. https://www.ama-assn.org/education/accelerating-change-medical-education/how-med-schools-are-preparing-students-team-based

American Psychological Association. (2017). *Guidelines for education and training at the doctoral and postdoctoral level in consulting psychology (CP)/organizational consulting psychology*. https://www.apa.org/about/policy/education-training.pdf

American Psychological Association. (2018). *Stress effects on the body*. https://www.apa.org/topics/stress/body#menu

American Psychological Association, APA Task Force on Race and Ethnicity Guidelines in Psychology. (2019). *APA guidelines on race and ethnicity in psychology*. https://www.apa.org/about/policy/guidelines-race-ethnicity.pdf

Angermuller, J. (2017). Academic careers and the valuation of academics. A discursive perspective on status categories and academic salaries in France as compared to the U.S., Germany and Great Britain. *Higher Education, 73*, 963–980. https://doi.org/10.1007/s10734-017-0117-1

Appelo, J. (2016). *Managing for happiness: Games, tools, and practices to motivate any team*. Wiley.

Artz, B., Goodall, A., & Oswald, A. J. (2016, December 29). If your boss could do your job, you're more likely to be happy at work. *Harvard Business Review*.

https://hbr.org/2016/12/if-your-boss-could-do-your-job-youre-more-likely-to-be-happy-at-work

Austin, H. M. (2016). Women in education, science and leadership in New Zealand: A personal reflection. *Studies in Higher Education, 41*(5), 914–919. https://doi.org/10.1080/03075079.2016.1147725

Bäcklander, G. (2019). Doing complexity leadership theory: How agile coaches at Spotify practise enabling leadership. *Creativity and Innovation Management, 28*(1), 42–60. https://doi.org/10.1111/caim.12303

Balser, J. R. (2019). The case for executive coaching in academic medicine. *Consulting Psychology Journal, 71*(3), 165–169. https://doi.org/10.1037/cpb0000133

Banerjee, P. M., & Cole, B. M. (2012). A study of biotechnology start-ups undergoing leadership change: Antecedents of change and endogenous performance consequences. *Technovation, 32*(9–10), 568–578. https://doi.org/10.1016/j.technovation.2012.05.003

Bang, H., & Midelfart, T. N. (2017). What characterizes effective management teams? A research-based approach. *Consulting Psychology Journal, 69*(4), 334–359. https://doi.org/10.1037/cpb0000098

Bass, B. M. (1990). *Bass & Stogdill's handbook of leadership* (3rd ed.). Free Press.

Beck, K., Beedle, M., van Bennekum, A., Cockburn, A., Cunningham, W., Fowler, M., Grenning, J., Highsmith, J., Hunt, A., Jeffries, R., Kern, J., Marick, B., Martin, R. C., Mellor, S., Schwaber, K., Sutherland, J., & Thomas, D. (2001). *Manifesto for Agile software development.* http://agilemanifesto.org/iso/en/manifesto.html

Behroozi, M., Shirolkar, S., Barik, T., & Parnin, C. (2020). Does stress impact technical interview performance? *ESEC/FSE 2020: Proceedings of the 28th ACM Joint Meeting on European Software Engineering Conference and Symposium on the Foundations of Software Engineering* (pp. 481–492). Association for Computing Machinery. https://doi.org/10.1145/3368089.3409712

Bellman, G. M. (1990). *The consultant's calling: Bringing who you are to what you do.* Jossey-Bass.

Bengtsson, M. (2016). How to plan and perform a qualitative study using content analysis. *NursingPlus Open, 2*, 8–14. https://doi.org/10.1016/j.npls.2016.01.001

Benson, K. (2016, November 8). *The anger iceberg.* The Gottman Institute. https://www.gottman.com/blog/the-anger-iceberg/

Berman, W. H. (2019). Coaching C-suite executives and business founders. *Consulting Psychology Journal, 71*(2), 72–85. https://doi.org/10.1037/cpb0000128

Bhatia, S., & Amati, J. P. (2010). "If these women can do it, I can do it, too": Building women engineering leaders through graduate peer mentoring. *Leadership and Management in Engineering, 10*(4), 174–184. https://doi.org/10.1061/(ASCE)LM.1943-5630.0000081

Bidwell, A. (2015, February 24). STEM workforce no more diverse than 14 years ago. *US News & World Report.* https://www.usnews.com/news/stem-solutions/articles/2015/02/24/stem-workforce-no-more-diverse-than-14-years-ago

Black, P. M. (2006). Challenges in contemporary academic neurosurgery. *Neurosurgery, 58*(3), 419–425. https://doi.org/10.1227/01.NEU.0000197139.61412.36

BlessingWhite. (2013, April). *Managing technical people—Leadership report* [White paper]. Engageforsuccess.org. https://blessingwhite.com/leading-technical-people-research-report/

Block, P. (2011). *Flawless consulting: A guide to getting your expertise used.* Pfeiffer.

Bonawandt, C., & Manganello, K. (2019, February 21). *Why engineers earn more.* https://www.thomasnet.com/insights/why-engineers-earn-more/

Booz, M. (2018, March 15). These 3 industries have the highest talent turnover rates. *LinkedIn Talent Blog.* https://business.linkedin.com/talent-solutions/blog/trends-and-research/2018/the-3-industries-with-the-highest-turnover-rates

Bradberry, T. (2012). *Leadership 2.0* (1st ed.). TalentSmart.

Bradberry, T., & Greaves, J. (2009). *Emotional intelligence 2.0.* TalentSmart.

Brahm, T., & Kunze, F. (2012). The role of trust climate in virtual teams. *Journal of Managerial Psychology, 27*(6), 595–614. https://doi.org/10.1108/02683941211252446

Briggs, B., Larmar, K., Kark, K., & Shaikh, A. (2018). *2018 global CIO survey: Manifesting legacy.* Deloitte Insights. https://www2.deloitte.com/us/en/insights/topics/leadership/global-cio-survey-2018.html

Britton, M. G. (2010). Engineering vs. science in the public eye. *Canadian Consulting Engineer, 51*(1), 31–32. https://www.canadianconsultingengineer.com/features/engineering-vs-science-in-the-public-eye/

Bryant, A. (2011, March 12). Google's 8-point plan to help managers improve. *The New York Times.* https://www.nytimes.com/2011/03/13/business/13hire.html?smid=pl-share

Cahill, T. F., & Sedrak, M. (2012). Leading a multigenerational workforce: Strategies for attracting and retaining millennials. *Frontiers of Health Services Management, 29*(1), 3–15. https://doi.org/10.1097/01974520-201207000-00002

Cappelli, P. (2019, May–June). Your approach to hiring is all wrong: Outsourcing and algorithms won't get you the people you need. *Harvard Business Review.* https://hbr.org/2019/05/your-approach-to-hiring-is-all-wrong

Carmichael, S. G. (2018). Why technical experts make great leaders [Audio podcast]. *Harvard Business Review.* https://hbr.org/podcast/2018/04/why-technical-experts-make-great-leaders

Castilla, E. J., & Benard, S. (2010). The paradox of meritocracy in organizations. *Administrative Science Quarterly, 55*(4), 543–676. https://doi.org/10.2189/asqu.2010.55.4.543

CB Insights. (2019, November 6). *The top 20 reasons startups fail.* https://www. cbinsights.com/research/startup-failure-reasons-top/

Chamorro-Premuzic, T. (2015, November 2). Why bad guys win at work. *Harvard Business Review.* https://hbr.org/2015/11/why-bad-guys-win-at-work

Charan, R., Drotter, S., & Noel, J. (2011). *The leadership pipeline: How to build the leadership powered company* (2nd ed.). Jossey-Bass.

Chaudhuri, S., & Alagaraja, M. (2014). An expatriate's perspective on leadership and leading (a global organization) in India: Interview with Matt Barney. *Human Resource Development International, 17*(3), 358–365. https://doi.org/ 10.1080/13678868.2014.896125

Chen, P. D., & Simpson, P. A. (2015). Does personality matter? Applying Holland's typology to analyze students' self-selection into science, technology, engineering, and mathematics majors. *The Journal of Higher Education, 86*(5), 725–750.

Cheryan, S., Ziegler, S. A., Montoya, A. K., & Jiang, L. (2017). Why are some STEM fields more gender balanced than others? *Psychological Bulletin, 143*(1), 1–35. https://doi.org/10.1037/bul0000052

Cisco Systems. (n.d.). *Cisco Systems corporate timeline.* https://newsroom.cisco. com/dlls/corporate_timeline_2008.pdf

Coe, I. R., Wiley, R., & Bekker, L.-G. (2019). Organisational best practices towards gender equality in science and medicine. *The Lancet, 393*(10171), 587–593. https://doi.org/10.1016/S0140-6736(18)33188-X

Connell, J. (2018, October 11). *Geoffrey Mattson: People strategies for techno-entitled nerds.* https://reinventingnerds.blubrry.net/2018/10/11/geoffrey-mattson-people-strategies-for-techno-entitled-nerds/

Connell, J. B., Sorenson, R. C., Robinson, K. L., & Ellis, S. J. (2003). Identifying successful telecommuters. In P. Isaías & N. Karmakar (Eds.), *Proceedings of the IADIS International Conference on WWW/Internet* (pp. 1098–1100). IADIS. http://www.iadisportal.org/wwwinternet-2003-proceedings

Covey, S. M. R. (2006). *The speed of trust.* Free Press.

Crabb, S. (2011). The use of coaching principles to foster employee engagement. *Coaching Psychologist, 7*(1), 27–34.

Crane, T. G. (2018). *The rise of the coachable leader.* FTA Press.

Crawford, E. R., LePine, J. A., & Rich, B. L. (2010). Linking job demands and resources to employee engagement and burnout: A theoretical extension and meta-analytic test. *Journal of Applied Psychology, 95*(5), 834–848. https://doi.org/ 10.1037/a0019364

Crayon, C., Patton, T., Gyurcsak, S. A., & Steigerwald, A. (2017). Managing a virtual project team: Offshoring technical services in the Philippines. *International Journal of Global Business, 10*(1), 37–46.

Crosby, G. (2021). *Planned change: Why Kurt Lewin's social science is still best practice for business results, change management, and human progress.* Routledge.

Dagi, T. F. (2017). Seven ethical issues affecting neurosurgeons in the context of health care reform. *Neurosurgery, 80*(4S), S83–S91. https://doi.org/10.1093/neuros/nyx017

Daly, P. (2014). In the minority: Not the usual computer science nerd. *Grand Rapids Business Journal, 32*(26), 8–9.

Daniels, C. B. (2009). Improving leadership in a technical environment: A case example of the ConITS Leadership Institute. *Engineering Management Journal, 21*(1), 47–52. https://doi.org/10.1080/10429247.2009.11431798

de Haan, E. (2019). A systematic review of qualitative studies in workplace and executive coaching: The emergence of a body of research. *Consulting Psychology Journal, 71*(4), 227–248. https://doi.org/10.1037/cpb0000144

Denning, S. (2018). The challenge of leadership in the age of Agile. *Leader to Leader, 2018*(89), 20–25. https://doi.org/10.1002/ltl.20371

Derue, D. S., Nahrgang, J. D., Wellman, N., & Humphrey, S. E. (2011). Trait and behavioral theories of leadership: An integration and meta-analytic test of their relative validity. *Personnel Psychology, 64*(1), 7–52. https://doi.org/10.1111/j.1744-6570.2010.01201.x

Desjardins, J. (2017, November 10). Here's how many millions of lines of code it takes to run different software. *Business Insider.* https://www.businessinsider.com/how-many-lines-of-code-it-takes-to-run-different-software-2017-2?international=true&r=US&IR=T

Deutsch, A. L. (2020, October 6). The 5 industries driving the U.S. economy. *Investopedia.* https://www.investopedia.com/articles/investing/042915/5-industries-driving-us-economy.asp

Development Dimensions International, Inc., The Conference Board Inc., & EYGM Limited. (2018, November 10). *Global leadership forecast 2018: 25 research insights to fuel your people strategy.* https://www.ddiworld.com/glf2018

DeVilbiss, C. E., & Gilbert, D. C. (2005). Resolve conflict to improve productivity. *Leadership and Management in Engineering, 5*(4), 87–91. https://doi.org/10.1061/(ASCE)1532-6748(2005)5:4(87)

Dietrich, A. (2004). The cognitive neuroscience of creativity. *Psychonomic Bulletin & Review, 11*(6), 1011–1026. https://doi.org/10.3758/BF03196731

Dodge, K. (2020, May 15). What is the benefit of an engineering degree vs a science degree? *DegreeQuery.* https://www.degreequery.com/what-is-the-benefit-of-an-engineering-degree-vs-a-science-degree/

Dutt, K. (2018, December 17). How implicit bias and lack of diversity undermine science. *Scientific American.* https://blogs.scientificamerican.com/voices/how-implicit-bias-and-lack-of-diversity-undermine-science/

Dye, C., & Garman, A. N. (2015). *Exceptional leadership: 16 critical competencies for healthcare executives* (2nd ed.). Health Administration Press.

Dyrbye, L. N., Burke, S. E., Hardeman, R. R., Herrin, J., Wittlin, N. M., Yeazel, M., Dovidio, J. F., Cunningham, B., White, R. O., Phelan, S. M., Satele, D. V., Shanafelt, T. D., & van Ryn, M. (2018). Association of clinical specialty with symptoms of burnout and career choice regret among US resident physicians [Replacement article with corrections highlighted]. *Journal of the American Medical Association, 320*(11), 1114–1130. https://doi.org/10.1001/jama.2018.12615

Eby, K. (2017, February 15). What's the difference? Agile vs Scrum vs Waterfall vs Kanban. *Smartsheet.* https://www.smartsheet.com/agile-vs-scrum-vs-waterfall-vs-kanban

Edmondson, D. R., Matthews, L. M., & Ambrose, S. C. (2019). A meta-analytic review of emotional exhaustion in a sales context. *Journal of Personal Selling & Sales Management, 39*(3), 275–286. https://doi.org/10.1080/08853134.2019.1592684

Emison, G. A. (2011). Transformative leadership for engineering in a time of complexity. *Leadership and Management in Engineering, 11*(2), 97–102. https://doi.org/10.1061/(ASCE)LM.1943-5630.0000108

Emler, N. (2019). Seven moral challenges of leadership. *Consulting Psychology Journal, 71*(1), 32–46. https://doi.org/10.1037/cpb0000136

Epstein, M. J., & Shelton, R. (2019). *The brilliant jerk conundrum: Thriving with and governing a dominant visionary.* Conundrum Press.

Ernst & Young. (2018). *The new age: Artificial intelligence for human resource opportunities and functions.* https://www.ey.com/Publication/vwLUAssets/EY-the-new-age-artificial-intelligence-for-human-resource-opportunities-and-functions/$FILE/EY-the-new-age-artificial-intelligence-for-human-resource-opportunities-and-functions.pdf

Eswaran, V. (2019, April 29). The business case for diversity is now overwhelming. Here's why. *World Economic Forum.* https://www.weforum.org/agenda/2019/04/business-case-for-diversity-in-the-workplace/

European Union. (2018, May 25). *General Data Protection Regulation.* The European Parliament and the Council of the European Union. https://gdpr-info.eu/

Federal Energy Regulatory Commission. (2020, September 14). *Enforcement & legal.* U.S. Federal Energy Regulatory Commission. https://www.ferc.gov/

Felder, W., Yang, S., & Pennotti, M. (2016, September). *RT-149: Leadership development framework for the technical acquisition workforce technical report SERC—2016—TR—111.* United States Department of Defense Stevens Institute of Technology Systems Engineering Research Center.

Ferdman, B. M. (2021). Inclusive leadership: The fulcrum of inclusion. In B. M. Ferdman, J. Prime, & R. E. Riggio (Eds.), *Inclusive leadership: Transforming diverse lives, workplaces, and societies* (pp. 3–24). Routledge.

Ferdman, B. M., Prime, J., & Riggio, R. E. (Eds.). (2021). *Inclusive leadership: Transforming diverse lives, workplaces, and societies*. Routledge.

Finkelstein, L. M., Costanza, D. P., & Goodwin, G. F. (2018). Do your high potentials have potential? The impact of individual differences and designation on leader success. *Personnel Psychology, 71*(1), 3–22. https://doi.org/10.1111/peps.12225

Fiske, S. T., Gilbert, D. T., & Lindzey, G. (Eds.). (2010). *Handbook of social psychology* (5th ed.). Wiley. https://doi.org/10.1002/9780470561119

Fogel, D. B. (2018). Factors associated with clinical trials that fail and opportunities for improving the likelihood of success: A review. *Contemporary Clinical Trials Communications, 11*, 156–164. https://doi.org/10.1016/j.conctc.2018.08.001

Forbes. (2020, April 7). *Forbes publishes 34th annual list of global billionaires.* https://www.forbes.com/sites/forbespr/2020/04/07/forbes-publishes-34th-annual-list-of-global-billionaires/

Fournier, C. (2017). *The manager's path: A guide for tech leaders navigating growth and change.* O'Reilly Media.

Frechtling, J. (2010). *The 2010 user-friendly handbook for project evaluations.* National Science Foundation Division of Research, Evaluation and Communication. https://www.purdue.edu/research/docs/pdf/2010NSFuser-friendly-handbookforprojectevaluation.pdf

Frese, M., & Gielnik, M. M. (2014). The psychology of entrepreneurship. *Annual Review of Organizational Psychology and Organizational Behavior, 1*(1), 413–438. https://doi.org/10.1146/annurev-orgpsych-031413-091326

Frye, L. (2018, June 1). *More people are taking time off, and that's good for business.* https://www.shrm.org/resourcesandtools/hr-topics/employee-relations/pages/workers-taking-more-vacation-.aspx

Fuhrmann, R. (2019, June 25). Stock exchanges around the world. *Investopedia.* https://www.investopedia.com/financial-edge/1212/stock-exchanges-around-the-world.aspx

Funk, C., & Parker, K. (2018, January 9). *Women and men in STEM often at odds over workplace equity.* Pew Research Center. https://www.pewsocialtrends.org/2018/01/09/women-and-men-in-stem-often-at-odds-over-workplace-equity/

Ganesh, R., Mahapatra, S., Fuehrer, D. L., Folkert, L. J., Jack, W. A., Jenkins, S. M., Bauer, B. A., Wahner-Roedler, D. L., & Sood, A. (2018). The stressed executive: Sources and predictors of stress among participants in an executive health program. *Global Advances in Health and Medicine, 7*, Article 2164956118806150. https://doi.org/10.1177/2164956118806150

Garvin, D. A. (2013, December). How Google sold its engineers on management. *Harvard Business Review*. https://hbr.org/2013/12/how-google-sold-its-engineers-on-management

Gautam, A., & Pan, X. (2016). The changing model of big pharma: Impact of key trends. *Drug Discovery Today, 21*(3), 379–384. https://doi.org/10.1016/j.drudis.2015.10.002

Gavet, M. (2021). *Trampled by unicorns: Big tech's empathy problem and how to fix it*. Wiley.

George, B. (2015). *Discover Your True North*. Jossey-Bass.

Geoui, T. (2016, September 14). *The importance of the team in drug development*. Elsevier. https://pharma.elsevier.com/chemistry/importance-team-drug-development/

Gibbs, K. (2014, September 10). Diversity in STEM: What it is and why it matters. *Scientific American*. https://blogs.scientificamerican.com/voices/diversity-in-stem-what-it-is-and-why-it-matters/

Glass, J. T. (2006). Leadership and teamwork in engineering. *Leader to Leader, 2006*(S1), 24–26. https://doi.org/10.1002/ltl.349

Goleman, D. (1994). *Emotional intelligence: Why it can matter more than IQ*. Bantam.

Gompers, P., & Kovvali, S. (2018). Finally, evidence that diversity improves financial performance. *Harvard Business Review*. https://hbr.org/2018/07/the-other-diversity-dividend

Google. (2020a). *re:Work—Introduction*. https://rework.withgoogle.com/guides/understanding-team-effectiveness/steps/introduction/

Google. (2020b). *re:Work—Managers*. https://rework.withgoogle.com/subjects/managers/

Gregory, J. B., & Levy, P. E. (2015). *Using feedback in organizational consulting*. American Psychological Association.

Gøtzsche-Astrup, O. (2018). The bright and dark sides of talent at work: A study of the personalities of talent development-program participants. *Consulting Psychology Journal, 70*(2), 167–181. https://doi.org/10.1037/cpb0000105

Greiner, L. E. (1998). Evolution and revolution as organizations grow. *Harvard Business Review, 76*(3), 55–60, 62–66, 68.

Grenny, J., & Maxfield, D. (2016, October 17). Leaders need different skills to thrive in tech. *Harvard Business Review*. https://hbr.org/2016/10/leaders-need-different-skills-to-thrive-in-tech

Gurdon, M. A., & Samsom, K. J. (2010). A longitudinal study of success and failure among scientist-started ventures. *Technovation, 30*(3), 207–214. https://doi.org/10.1016/j.technovation.2009.10.004

Gustavsson, T. (2019). Changes over time in a planned inter-team coordination routine. In R. Hoda (Ed.), *Agile processes in software engineering and extreme programming—Workshops. XP 2019. Lecture Notes in Business Information Processing* (Vol. 364, pp. 105–111). Springer. https://doi.org/10.1007/978-3-030-30126-2_13

Hambley, C. (2020). CONNECT©: A brain-friendly model for leaders and organizations. *Consulting Psychology Journal, 72*(3), 168–197. https://doi.org/10.1037/cpb0000187

Hammonds, K. H. (2005, August). *Why we hate HR.* Fast Company. https://www.fastcompany.com/53319/why-we-hate-hr

Heifetz, R. A., & Linsky, M. (2009). *The practice of adaptive leadership: Tools and tactics for changing your organization and the world.* Harvard Business School Press.

Hess, D. W. (2018). *Leadership by engineers and scientists: Professional skills needed to succeed in a changing world.* Wiley. https://doi.org/10.1002/9781119436553

Hiltzik, M. (2018, February 1). Column: A gender discrimination case at the legendary Salk Institute exposes an ugly problem in science. *The Los Angeles Times.* https://www.latimes.com/business/hiltzik/la-fi-hiltzik-salk-discrimination-20180202-story.html

Hogg, M. A., van Knippenberg, D., & Rast, D. E., III. (2012). Intergroup leadership in organizations: Leading across group and organizational boundaries. *Academy of Management Review, 37*(2), 232–255. https://doi.org/10.5465/amr.2010.0221

Hoving, R. (2007). Information technology leadership challenges—Past, present, and future. *Information Systems Management, 24*(2), 147–153. https://doi.org/10.1080/10580530701221049

Huber, G. P. (2011). Organizations: Theory, design, future. In S. Zedeck (Ed.), *APA handbook of industrial and organizational psychology: Vol. 1. Building and developing the organization* (pp. 117–160). American Psychological Association. https://doi.org/10.1037/12169-005

Hurd, J. L. (2009). Development coaching: Helping scientific and technical professionals make the leap into leadership. *Global Business and Organizational Excellence, 28*(5), 39–51. https://doi.org/10.1002/joe.20277

Ihsan, Z., & Furnham, A. (2018). The new technologies in personality assessment: A review. *Consulting Psychology Journal, 70*(2), 147–166. https://doi.org/10.1037/cpb0000106

Isaacson, W. (2014). *The innovators: How a group of hackers, geniuses and geeks created the digital revolution.* Simon and Schuster.

Jack, A. I., Dawson, A. J., Begany, K. L., Leckie, R. L., Barry, K. P., Ciccia, A. H., & Snyder, A. Z. (2013, February 1). fMRI reveals reciprocal inhibition between social and physical cognitive domains. *NeuroImage, 66,* 385–401. https://doi.org/10.1016/j.neuroimage.2012.10.061

Jauk, E., Eberhardt, L., Koschmieder, C., Diedrich, J., Pretsch, J., Benedek, M., & Neubauer, A. C. (2019). A new measure for the assessment of appreciation for creative personality. *Creativity Research Journal, 31*(2), 149–163. https://doi.org/10.1080/10400419.2019.1606622

Johns, M. E. (2019). Lessons learned from decades of leading academic health centers. *Consulting Psychology Journal, 71*(3), 161–164. https://doi.org/10.1037/cpb0000135

Jøsok, Ø., Lugo, R., Knox, B. J., Sütterlin, S., & Helkala, K. (2019). Self-regulation and cognitive agility in cyber operations. *Frontiers in Psychology, 10*, Article 875. https://doi.org/10.3389/fpsyg.2019.00875

Kaiser Family Foundation. (2020, May 20). *Total number of nurse practitioners, by gender.* https://www.kff.org/other/state-indicator/total-number-of-nurse-practitioners-by-gender/?dataView=1¤tTimeframe=0&selectedRows=%7B%22wrapups%22%3A%7B%22united-states%22%3A%7B%7D%7D%7D&sortModel=%7B%22colId%22%3A%22Location%22%2C%22sort%22%3A%22asc%22%7D

Kaminsky, J. B. (2012). Impact of nontechnical leadership practices on IT project success. *Journal of Leadership Studies, 6*(1), 30–49. https://doi.org/10.1002/jls.21226

Kark, K., Briggs, B., Terzioglu, A., & Puranik, M. (2019, June 10). *The future of work in technology* [White paper]. Deloitte Insights. https://www2.deloitte.com/us/en/insights/focus/technology-and-the-future-of-work/tech-leaders-reimagining-work-workforce-workplace.html

Kark, K., Phillips, A. N., Briggs, B., Lillie, M., Tweardy, J., & Buchholz, S. (2020). *The kinetic leader: Boldly reinventing the enterprise* [White paper]. Deloitte. https://www2.deloitte.com/us/en/insights/topics/leadership/global-technology-leadership-study.html.html

Kendra, K. A., & Taplin, L. J. (2004). Change agent competencies for information technology project managers. *Consulting Psychology Journal, 56*(1), 20–34. https://doi.org/10.1037/1061-4087.56.1.20

Khan, B., Robbins, C., & Okrent, A. (2020, January). *The state of U.S. science and engineering 2020.* National Science Foundation. https://ncses.nsf.gov/pubs/nsb20201/u-s-s-e-workforce

Kahneman, D. (2013, March/April). What really matters? *Psychotherapy Networker, 39*, 50.

Kleinman, V. (2017, May 26). *Big pharma: From siloed to streamlined.* Life Science Leader. https://www.lifescienceleader.com/doc/big-pharma-from-siloed-to-streamlined-0001

Kornfield, M., Rowland, C., Bernstein, L., & Barrett, D. (2020, October 21). Purdue Pharma agrees to plead guilty to federal criminal charges in settlement over opioid crisis. *The Washington Post.* https://www.washingtonpost.com/national-security/2020/10/21/purdue-pharma-charges/

KPMG. (2020). *The future of HR 2020: Which path are you taking?* https://home.kpmg/xx/en/home/insights/2019/11/the-future-of-human-resources-2020.html

Kumar, S., & Hsiao, J. K. (2007). Engineers learn "soft skills the hard way": Planting a seed of leadership in engineering classes. *Leadership and Management in Engineering, 7*(1), 18–23. https://doi.org/10.1061/(ASCE)1532-6748(2007)7:1(18)

Lagasse, J. (2021, January 25). Physician happiness plunges in new healthcare burnout report. *Healthcare Finance.* https://www.healthcarefinancenews.com/news/physician-happiness-plunges-new-healthcare-burnout-report

Lamb, R., Annetta, L., Vallett, D., Firestone, J., Schmitter-Edgecombe, M., Walker, H., Deviller, N., & Hoston, D. (2018). Psychosocial factors impacting STEM career selection. *The Journal of Educational Research, 111*(4), 446–458. https://doi.org/10.1080/00220671.2017.1295359

Landis, E. A., Hill, D., & Harvey, M. R. (2014). A synthesis of leadership theories and styles. *Journal of Management Policies and Practices, 15*(2), 97–100.

Lauring, J., & Jonasson, C. (2018). Can leadership compensate for deficient inclusiveness in global virtual teams? *Human Resource Management Journal, 28*(3), 392–409. https://doi.org/10.1111/1748-8583.12184

Leadem, R. (2017, November 6). *The 15 tech companies with the highest signing bonuses.* Entrepreneur. https://www.entrepreneur.com/slideshow/304043

Lencioni, P. (2002). *The five dysfunctions of a team.* Jossey-Bass.

Leonard, H. S. (2017). A teachable approach to leadership. *Consulting Psychology Journal, 69*(4), 243–266. https://doi.org/10.1037/cpb0000096

Leonardi, P., & Contractor, N. (2018, November–December). Better people analytics: Measure who they know, not just who they are. *Harvard Business Review.* https://hbr.org/2018/11/better-people-analytics

Levitt, H. M. (2019). *Reporting qualitative research in psychology: How to meet APA style journal article reporting standards.* American Psychological Association. https://doi.org/10.1037/0000121-000

Litman, J. (2018, May 16). *Empathy in medical education: Can kindness be taught?* The Public Health Advocate. https://pha.berkeley.edu/2018/05/16/empathy-in-medical-education-can-kindness-be-taught/

Lorenzo, R., Voigt, N., Tsusaka, M., Krentz, M., & Abouzahr, K. (2018, January 23). *How diverse leadership teams boost innovation* [White paper]. Boston Consulting Group. https://www.bcg.com/en-us/publications/2018/how-diverse-leadership-teams-boost-innovation

Loria, K. (2019, September 4). The future of healthcare leadership. *Managed Healthcare Executive*. https://www.managedhealthcareexecutive.com/view/ future-healthcare-leadership

Lowman, R. L. (2016). *An introduction to consulting psychology: Working with individuals, groups, and organizations*. American Psychological Association. https://doi.org/10.1037/14853-000

Luse, A., McElroy, J. C., Townsend, A. M., & DeMarie, S. (2013). Personality and cognitive style as predictors of preference for working in virtual teams. *Computers in Human Behavior, 29*(4), 1825–1832. https://doi.org/10.1016/ j.chb.2013.02.007

Madhusoodanan, J. (2014, November 1). 2014 Life sciences salary survey. *The Scientist*. https://www.the-scientist.com/features/2014-life-sciences-salary- survey-36509

Mann, A. (2018, January 15). *Why we need best friends at work*. Gallup. https:// www.gallup.com/workplace/236213/why-need-best-friends-work.aspx

Markman, A. (2017, November 15). Can you be a great leader without technical expertise? *Harvard Business Review*. https://hbr.org/2017/11/can-you-be-a- great-leader-without-technical-expertise

Martin, G., Beech, N., MacIntosh, R., & Bushfield, S. (2015). Potential challenges facing distributed leadership in health care: Evidence from the UK National Health Service. *Service Sociology of Health & Illness, 37*(1), 14–29. https://doi.org/ 10.1111/1467-9566.12171

Martino, K. (2018). A leadership model for technical people. *Industrial management, 60*(6), 19–24. http://keithmartino.com/wp-content/uploads/2018/ 12/Industrial-Management-Magazine-A-Leadership-Model-Original- Dec11a2018.pdf

Mathieu, J. E., Hollenbeck, J. R., van Knippenberg, D., & Ilgen, D. R. (2017). A century of work teams in the *Journal of Applied Psychology. Journal of Applied Psychology, 102*(3), 452–467. https://doi.org/10.1037/apl0000128

Mayo Clinic Staff. (2021). *Job burnout: How to spot it and take action*. https://www. mayoclinic.org/healthy-lifestyle/adult-health/in-depth/burnout/art-20046642

McKay, A. S., Reiter-Palmon, R., & Kaufman, J. C. (2020). *Creative success in teams*. Academic Press.

Meagher, B. R., & Cheadle, A. D. (2020). Distant from others, but close to home: The relationship between home attachment and mental health during COVID-19. *Journal of Environmental Psychology, 72*, Article 101516. https://doi.org/ 10.1016/j.jenvp.2020.101516

Moody, J. (2019, January 24). A guide to STEM majors. *U.S. News & World Report*. https://www.usnews.com/education/best-colleges/articles/2019-01-24/ a-guide-to-stem-majors

Morris, Z. (2019, June 14). *What's driving the tech sector's extreme turnover rate?* InformationWeek. https://www.informationweek.com/strategic-cio/team-building-and-staffing/whats-driving-the-tech-sectors-extreme-turnover-rate/a/d-id/1334920

Mundy, L. (2017, April). Why is Silicon Valley so awful to women? *The Atlantic.* https://www.theatlantic.com/magazine/archive/2017/04/why-is-silicon-valley-so-awful-to-women/517788/

Murray, E. (2020, October 9). The next generation of office communication tech. *Harvard Business Review.* https://hbr.org/2020/10/the-next-generation-of-office-communication-tech

Nadella, S., Shaw, G., & Nichols, J. T. (2017). *Hit refresh: The quest to rediscover Microsoft's soul and imagine a better future for everyone.* Harper Business.

National Human Genome Research Institute. (2019, March 13). *Human Genome Project FAQ.* https://www.genome.gov/human-genome-project/Completion-FAQ

Nauta, M. M. (2010). The development, evolution, and status of Holland's theory of vocational personalities: Reflections and future directions for counseling psychology. *Journal of Counseling Psychology, 57*(1), 11–22. https://doi.org/10.1037/a0018213

Nemeth, C. J., Personnaz, B., Personnaz, M., & Goncalo, J. A. (2004). The liberating role of conflict in group creativity: A study in two countries. *European Journal of Social Psychology, 34*(4), 365–374. https://doi.org/10.1002/ejsp.210

Nummenmaa, L., Glerean, E., Hari, R., & Hietanen, J. K. (2014). Bodily maps of emotions. *Proceedings of the National Academy of Sciences of the United States of America, 111*(2), 646–651. https://doi.org/10.1073/pnas.1321664111

Nunn, R., O'Donnell, J., & Shambaugh, J. (2018, October). *A dozen facts about immigration.* The Hamilton Project. https://www.hamiltonproject.org/papers/a_dozen_facts_about_immigration

O'Flaherty, K. (2020, November 29). Microsoft's new productivity score and workplace tracking: Here's the problem. *Forbes.* https://www.forbes.com/sites/kateoflahertyuk/2020/11/29/microsofts-new-productivity-score-what-does-it-mean-for-you/?sh=6622cf941d6f

Ortiz de Guinea, A., Webster, J., & Staples, D. S. (2012). A meta-analysis of the consequences of virtualness on team functioning. *Information & Management, 49*(6), 301–308. https://doi.org/10.1016/j.im.2012.08.003

Pandya, K. D. (2014). The key competencies of project leader beyond the essential technical capabilities. *IUP Journal of Knowledge Management, 12*, 39–48. https://papers.ssrn.com/sol3/papers.cfm?abstract_id=2637233

Pattanaik, A. (2014, May 5–7). *Complexity of project management in the pharmaceutical industry* [Paper presentation]. PMI® Global Congress 2014, EMEA, Dubai, United Arab Emirates.

Patterson, K., Grenny, J., McMillan, R., & Switzler, A. (2002). *Crucial conversations*. McGraw-Hill.

PayScale. (2020). *Companies with the most and least loyal employees: Full list of most and least loyal employees* [White paper]. https://www.payscale.com/data-packages/employee-loyalty/full-list

Perez, E. (2019). *Top 5 most popular startup sectors*. UCI Beall Applied Innovation. http://innovation.uci.edu/2019/07/top-5-most-popular-startup-sectors/

Petrou, P., Linden, D., Mainemelis, C., & Salcescu, O. C. (2020). Rebel with a cause: When does employee rebelliousness relate to creativity? *Journal of Occupational and Organizational Psychology, 93*(4), 811–833. https://doi.org/10.1111/joop.12324

Rasoal, C., Danielsson, H., & Jungert, T. (2012). Empathy among students in engineering programmes. *European Journal of Engineering Education, 37*(5), 427–435. https://doi.org/10.1080/03043797.2012.708720

Rathmell, W. K., Brown, N. J., & Kilburg, R. R. (2019). Transformation to academic leadership: The role of mentorship and executive coaching. *Consulting Psychology Journal, 71*(3), 141–160. https://doi.org/10.1037/cpb0000124

Redden, E. (2018, February 19). Is econ STEM? *Inside Higher Ed.* https://www.insidehighered.com/admissions/article/2018/02/19/economics-departments-reclassify-their-programs-stem-attract-and-help

Reh, G. (2020). *2020 global life sciences outlook: Creating new value, building blocks for the future* [White paper]. Deloitte Insights. https://documents.deloitte.com/insights/2020globallifesciencesoutlook

Reina, C. S., Rogers, K. M., Peterson, S. J., Byron, K., & Hom, P. W. (2017). Quitting the boss? The role of manager influence tactics and employee emotional engagement in voluntary turnover. *Journal of Leadership & Organizational Studies, 25*(1), 5–18. https://doi.org/10.1177/1548051817709007

Rigby, D. K., Elk, S., & Berez, S. (2020, April 14). The Agile C-suite. *Harvard Business Review.* https://hbr.org/2020/05/the-agile-c-suite

Rigby, D. K., Sutherland, J., & Takeuchi, H. (2016, May). Embracing Agile. *Harvard Business Review.* https://hbr.org/2016/05/embracing-agile?autocomplete=true19

Ringel, M., Baeza, R., Grassl, F., Panandiker, R., & Harnoss, J. (2020, June). *The most innovative companies 2020: The serial innovation imperative* [White paper]. Boston Consulting Group. https://image-src.bcg.com/Images/BCG-Most-Innovative-Companies-2020-Jun-2020-R-4_tcm9-251007.pdf

Rook, C., Hellwig, T., Florent-Treacy, E., & Kets de Vries, M. (2019). Workplace stress in senior executives: Coaching the "uncoachable." *International Coaching Psychology Review, 14*(2), 7–23.

Roth, L. J. (2020). *Digital transformation: An executive guide to survive and thrive in the new economy*. Balboa Press.

Rounds, J., Hoff, K., & Lewis, P. (Eds.). (2021). *O*NET® interest profiler manual.* U.S. Department of Labor. https://www.onetcenter.org/reports/IP_Manual.html

Royce, W. (1970). *Managing the development of large software systems.* http://www-scf.usc.edu/~csci201/lectures/Lecture11/royce1970.pdf

Salicru, S. (2020). A new model of leadership-as-practice development for consulting psychologists. *Consulting Psychology Journal, 72*(2), 79–99. https://doi.org/10.1037/cpb0000142

Sánchez-Ruiz, M. J., Pérez-González, J. C., & Petrides, K. V. (2010). Trait emotional intelligence profiles of students from different university faculties. *Australian Journal of Psychology, 62*(1), 51–57. https://doi.org/10.1080/00049530903312907

Sansone, C., & Schreiber-Abshire, W. (2011). A rare and valued asset: Developing leaders for research, scientific, technology and engineering organizations. *Organization Development Journal, 29*(2), 47–57.

Sato, W. (2016). Scientists' personality, values, and well-being. *SpringerPlus, 5*(1), 613. https://doi.org/10.1186/s40064-016-2225-2

Schwab, D. (2018, August 25). *Salk Institute settles discrimination suit with majority of parties.* SDNews.Com. http://www.sdnews.com/view/full_story/27594793/article-Salk-Institute-settles-discrimination-suit-with-majority-of-parties?instance=bbp

Scott, K. (2019). *Radical candor: Be a kick-ass boss without losing your humanity.* St. Martin's Press.

Silzer, R., & Church, A. H. (2009). The pearls and perils of identifying potential. *Industrial and Organizational Psychology, 2*(4), 377–412. https://doi.org/10.1111/j.1754-9434.2009.01163.x

Socconini, L., & Reato, C. (2018). *Lean Six Sigma management system: Breakthrough results step by step (Lean Six Sigma Certification).* Luis Socconini.

Solon, O. (2017, November 8). Ashamed to work in Silicon Valley: How techies became the new bankers. *The Guardian.* https://www.theguardian.com/technology/2017/nov/08/ashamed-to-work-in-silicon-valley-how-techies-became-the-new-bankers

Sorenson, R. C., Robinson, K. L., Connell, J. B., & Ellis, S. J. (2003, October 4–11). *Factors affecting the success of telework: A collection of case studies* [Paper presentation]. International Conference on Advances in the Internet, Processing, Systems, and Interdisciplinary Research Conference, Sveti Stefan, Montenegro.

Sousa, C., & Luís, C. (2013). Innovation, creativity and reward practices in academic spin-offs: The case of the IST Spin-off Community. *Portuguese Journal of Social Science, 12*(3), 263–286. https://doi.org/10.1386/pjss.12.3.263_1

Stahl, A. (2020, July 21). *10 steps businesses can take to improve diversity and inclusion in the workforce.* Forbes. https://www.forbes.com/sites/ashleystahl/

2020/07/21/10-steps-businesses-can-take-to-improve-diversity-and-inclusion-in-the-workforce/#757264fa343e

Stankiewicz, K. (2020, December 4). *Heated on-air CNBC exchange between Sorkin and Santelli mirrors national debate over Covid lockdowns.* CNBC. https://www.cnbc.com/2020/12/04/cnbcs-andrew-ross-sorkin-rick-santelli-debate-over-covid-lockdowns.html

Steedman, M., Stockbridge, M., Taylor, K., & Cruz, M. (2020, January 24). *Ten years on: Measuring the return from pharmaceutical innovation 2019* [White paper]. DeLoitte. https://www2.deloitte.com/us/en/pages/life-sciences-and-health-care/articles/measuring-return-from-pharmaceutical-innovation.html

Stellman, A., & Greene, J. (2013). *Learning Agile: Understanding Scrum, XP, Lean, and Kanban* (1st ed.). O'Reilly Media.

Sternberg, R. J. (1999). *Handbook of creativity.* Cambridge University Press.

Stoller, J. K., Goodall, A., & Baker, A. (2016, December 27). Why the best hospitals are managed by doctors. *Harvard Business Review.* https://hbr.org/2016/12/why-the-best-hospitals-are-managed-by-doctors.html

Strobel, J., Hess, J., Pan, R., & Wachter Morris, C. A. (2013). Empathy and care within engineering: Qualitative perspectives from engineering faculty and practicing engineers. *Engineering Studies, 5*(2), 137–159. https://doi.org/10.1080/19378629.2013.814136

Tuckman, B. W. (1965). Developmental sequence in small groups. *Psychological Bulletin, 63*(6), 384–399. https://doi.org/10.1037/h0022100

Turner-Moffatt, C. (2019). The power of mentorship: Strengthening women in leadership roles. *Professional Safety, 64*(8), 17–19.

U.S. Department of Health and Human Services. (2017, June 16). *Health information privacy.* https://www.hhs.gov/hipaa/for-professionals/index.html

U.S. Food and Drug Administration. (2018, June 18). *Learn about drug and device approvals.* https://www.fda.gov/patients/learn-about-drug-and-device-approvals

Van den Berg, G., & Pietersma, P. (2014). *Key management models: The 75+ models every manager needs to know* (3rd ed.). Pearson.

Vieth, C. S., & Smith, T. W. (2008). Engineering and technical leadership development: Challenges in a rapidly changing global market. *Chief Learning Officer, 7*(2), 46–49. https://www.chieflearningofficer.com/2008/02/01/engineering-and-technical-leadership-development-challenges-in-a-rapidly-changing-global-market/

Wai, J., Lubinski, D., & Benbow, C. P. (2009). Spatial ability for STEM domains: Aligning over 50 years of cumulative psychological knowledge solidifies its importance. *Journal of Educational Psychology, 101*(4), 817–835. https://doi.org/10.1037/a0016127

Walker, B. J. (2019). Coaching surgeons and emergency-room physicians. *Consulting Psychology Journal, 71*(2), 120–129. https://doi.org/10.1037/cpb0000130

White, E. (2009, April 7). How to increase workplace diversity. *The Wall Street Journal.* https://www.wsj.com/articles/BL-HOWTOMB-9

Why should I care about diversity in engineering? (2020, July/August). *PE Magazine.* https://www.nspe.org/resources/pe-magazine/july-2020/why-should-i-care-about-diversity-engineering#:%7E:text=There%20are%20many%20reasons.,a%20stronger%2C%20more%20unified%20profession.&text=In%20the%20past%2C%20the%20profession,almost%20exclusively%20white%2C%20male%20workforce

Williams, J. S., & Lowman, R. L. (2018). The efficacy of executive coaching: An empirical investigation of two approaches using random assignment and a switching-replications design. *Consulting Psychology Journal, 70*(3), 227–249. https://doi.org/10.1037/cpb0000115

Women's Bureau, U.S. Department of Labor. (2018). *Women in the labor force.* https://www.dol.gov/agencies/wb/data/facts-over-time/women-in-the-labor-force#womenstem

Wouters, O. J., McKee, M., & Luyten, J. (2020). Estimated research and development investment needed to bring a new medicine to market, 2009–2018. *Journal of the American Medical Association, 323*(9), 844–853. https://doi.org/10.1001/jama.2020.1166

Zielinski, D. (2019, December 4). People analytics software is changing the HR game: Next-generation people analytics software can help HR improve the gathering, correlating and analyzing of key data. *SHRM HR Magazine.* https://www.shrm.org/hr-today/news/hr-magazine/winter2019/pages/what-you-need-to-know-about-hr-people-analytics-software.aspx

Index

About the Author

Joanie B. Connell, PhD, is an organizational consultant who specializes in assessing and developing technical leaders. She earned a bachelor's degree in electrical engineering from Harvard College and a doctorate in psychology from the University of California Berkeley with an emphasis in industrial/organizational psychology. She has been consulting and teaching at the university level for over 20 years in organizational psychology, but prior to that she was a practicing electrical engineer in Silicon Valley for 8 years. Dr. Connell heads her own consulting firm, Flexible Work Solutions, which she founded in 2005 to provide consulting services in leadership assessment, development, and retention, primarily of technical employees. She consults with clients from startups to Fortune 100 companies in high tech, biotech, finance, legal, and many other industries. She hosts a podcast called "Reinventing Nerds," where she interviews technical leaders about their challenges and successes with developing people skills. She also works with younger generations, has a blog called "Lessons From the Workplace," and is the author of the book *Flying Without a Helicopter: How to Prepare Young People for Work and Life* (2015). All of this can be found on her company's website at https://flexibleworksolutions.com/.